The American Wilderness

in the words of
John Muir

"John the Baptist was not more eager to get all his fellow sinners into the Jordan than I to baptize all of mine in the beauty of God's mountains."

Mt. Morrison, California Sierra.

The American Wilderness

in the words of
John Muir

By the Editors of Country Beautiful

Publisher & Editorial Director: Michael P. Dineen
Executive Editor: Robert L. Polley
Edited by Kent Dannen

Photography by Ed Cooper

with additional photographs by David Muench, Kent Dannen and others

Country Beautiful
Waukesha, Wisconsin

"Any fool can destroy trees."

COUNTRY BEAUTIFUL: *Publisher and Editorial Director:* Michael P. Dineen; *Executive Editor:* Robert L. Polley; *Senior Editors:* Kenneth L. Schmitz; James H. Robb; *Art Director:* Buford Nixon; *Managing Editor:* John M. Nuhn; *Contributing Editor:* Kent Dannen; *Associate Editors:* D'Arlyn Marks; Kay Kundinger; *Editorial Assistant:* Nancy Backes; *Production Manager:* Donna Griesemer; *Editorial Secretary:* Jane Boyd; *Administration:* Brett E. Gries, Bruce Schneider; *Administrative Secretary:* Kathleen M. Stoner.

Country Beautiful Corporation is a wholly owned subsidiary of Flick-Reedy Corporation: *President:* Frank Flick; *Vice President and General Manager:* Michael P. Dineen; *Treasurer and Secretary:* August Caamano.

All photographs by Ed Cooper except where noted.

Frontispiece: *Pine trees in winter on east slope of Sierra.*

Dannen

6

CONTENTS

"... if a war of races should occur between the wild beasts and Lord Man I would be tempted to sympathize with the bears."

INTRODUCTION

Scotch immigrant John Muir wrote that there are "only two subjects on which Scotchmen get much excited, namely, religion and politics." Muir's whole life was shaped by his excitement over a Christianity that included a love of nature. His excitement over religion led him into exciting political crusades to save wilderness beauty, which he called "Nature's Bible." He taught Americans to hear "sermons in stones, storms, trees, flowers and animals." From the writings of this prophet of wilderness preservation comes much of the inspiration for America's rapidly expanding concern for the natural environment.

Muir's main influence came through his articles and books about his personal experiences in the wilds, especially in the Far West and Alaska. Throughout these narratives he wove his philosophy of wilderness values; his ideas are basically his own interpretation of Biblical teachings. Muir's complete familiarity with the Bible began during early childhood in Dunbar, Scotland: "Father made me learn so many Bible verses every day that by the time I was eleven years of age I had about three-fourths of the Old Testament and all of the New by heart and by sore flesh."

A faith based on individual interpretation of the Bible was a basic belief in the Disciples of Christ, a new ecumenical group which Daniel Muir joined. Formed on the American frontier by another Scot, Alexander Campbell, the Disciples influenced John Muir's father to leave a thriving business in 1849 and move his family to the New World.

The Muirs ended up on the Wisconsin frontier where their pioneer life was a hard one. John later wrote of the hostile attitude toward wilderness that hardship produced in their neighbors: "In the blindness of hunger, the early settlers, claiming Heaven as their guide, regarded God's trees as only a larger kind of pernicious weed, extremely hard to get rid of." However, John Muir's father taught his eight children that nature showed forth the glory and power of God, thus allowing John to see beyond the normal frontier prejudices against wilderness.

But Daniel Muir's religious attitudes usually were harsh and his behavior often inconsistent with the Biblical standard of love. John rebelled from his father's personal faith and, in the process, became disenchanted with the relatively liberal Disciples and all other organized churches. All his adult life Muir worshipped in temples of nature. God himself was the preacher; trees and wildlife together with Muir constituted the congregation.

After leaving home John Muir made his way in the world by means of his great inventive skill, which was something of a campus marvel during the four years he attended Wisconsin University. He never earned a degree, but instead transferred to the "University of the Wilderness." His wanderings in the wild both were supported by and distracted by inventing. In 1867, an accident while he was providing his skills to an Indianapolis carriage shop blinded him. Fearing that his loss of sight was permanent, Muir grieved over the time he had wasted inventing when he could have been learning from nature. After his recovery, he wasted no time: "As soon as I got into heaven's light, ... I bade adieu to mechanical inventions, determined to devote my life to the study of the inventions of God."

This study began with a thousand-mile botanical walk to the Gulf of Mexico. He then set sail for California and the Sierra Nevada Mountains. These rugged peaks, especially around Yosemite Valley, enthralled Muir for the rest of his life. But he was distressed by the despoilation of the Sierras in the name of material gain.

In 1871, three years after his arrival in California, he published the first of his conservation articles, urging the protection of Yosemite. It was the beginning of a crusade that climaxed with the establishment of Yosemite National Park in 1890. To protect this and other legislative gains, he organized the Sierra Club in 1892 and served as its president until his death in 1914.

Unfortunately, Muir lost the last big conservation battle of his life — the futile struggle to save the beautiful Hetch Hetchy Valley from being drowned as an unnecessary reservoir for San Francisco. Although he was deeply disappointed, Muir could console an ally that "the conscience of the whole country has been aroused from sleep." Out of the lost battle to save Hetch Hetchy was born a national movement for wilderness preservation. Today this movement and the wilderness beauty it defends stand as monuments to the prophetic vision and labor of John Muir.

- Kent Dannen

Opposite: *Cloud's Rest Peak rising behind Merced River in Yosemite.*

Boyhood and Youth

At a Sierra Club dinner toward the end of his life, John Muir became engaged in a conversation with another famous explorer about the value of nature in the moral education of children. Soon the two explorers were the only ones conversing as everyone else at the dinner listened with complete attention to the dialogue.

Agreeing that exposure to nature could be the most important factor in character development, Muir went on to maintain that a boy's reaction to nature was instinctively violent. But, "under proper training," he continued, "even the most savage boy will rise above the bloody flesh and sport business." As the boy each day was guided to a deeper understanding, the urge to kill was transfigured into love. Probably Muir was thinking of the book he had just written about his own upbringing, *The Story of My Boyhood and Youth.*

This book reveals how Muir's father tried to give his children a strong religious faith, but himself set a poor example. Naturally narrow-minded anyway, Daniel Muir could not see that his overbearing acquisitiveness constantly led him astray from Bible teachings. John often used the Bible knowledge his father literally had beaten into him to dispute his father's own ideas or actions.

But *Boyhood and Youth,* from which all the quotations in this chapter are taken, shows that Daniel Muir's efforts at religious education were saved from futility by the Wisconsin wilderness. The Biblical doctrine that nature shows forth the glory of God made a permanent impression on John. As he grew up, he saw Bible teachings restated all around him in nature. The wilderness gave John Muir the example of a loving and meaningful religion which his father failed to provide.

Opposite: *Deep understanding of nature requires a close scrutiny of the details of nature.*

Opposite: *Where the sea and the sky, the waves and the clouds are mingled together as one.*

When I was a boy in Scotland I was fond of everything that was wild, and all my life I've been growing fonder and fonder of wild places and wild creatures. Fortunately around my native town of Dunbar, by the stormy North Sea, there was no lack of wildness, though most of the land lay in smooth cultivation. With red-blooded playmates, wild as myself, I loved to wander in the fields to hear the birds sing, and along the seashore to gaze and wonder at the shells and seaweeds, eels and crabs in the pools among the rocks when the tide was low; and best of all to watch the waves in awful storms thundering on the black headlands and craggy ruins of the old Dunbar Castle when the sea and the sky, the waves and the clouds, were mingled together as one. We never thought of playing truant, but after I was five or six years old I ran away to the seashore or the fields almost every Saturday, and every day in the school vacations except Sundays, though solemnly warned that I must play at home in the garden and back yard, lest I should learn to think bad thoughts and say bad words. All in vain. In spite of the sure sore punishments that followed like shadows, the natural inherited wildness in our blood ran true on its glorious course as invincible and unstoppable as stars.

My earliest recollections of the country were gained on short walks with my grandfather when I was perhaps not over three years old. On one of these walks grandfather took me to Lord Lauderdale's gardens, where I saw figs growing against a sunny wall and tasted some of them, and got as many apples to eat as I wished. On another memorable walk in a hayfield, when we sat down to rest on one of the haycocks I heard a sharp, prickly, stinging cry, and, jumping up eagerly, called grandfather's attention to it. He said he heard only the wind, but I insisted on digging into the hay and turning it over until we discovered the source of the strange exciting sound — a mother field mouse with half a dozen naked young hanging to her teats. This to me was a wonderful discovery. No hunter could have been more excited on discovering a bear and her cubs in a wilderness den.

[F]ather made me learn so many Bible verses every day that by the time I was eleven years of age I had about three fourths of the Old Testament and all of the New by heart and by sore flesh. I could recite the New Testament from the beginning of Matthew to the end of Revelation without a single stop. The dangers of cramming and of making scholars study at home instead of letting their little brains rest were never heard of in those days. We carried our school-books home in a strap every night and committed to memory our next day's lessons before we went to bed, and to do that we had to bend our attention as closely on our tasks as lawyers on great million-dollar cases. I can't conceive of anything that would now enable me to concentrate my attention more fully than when I was a mere stripling boy, and it was all done by whipping — thrashing in general. Old-fashioned Scotch teachers spent no time in seeking short roads to knowledge, or in trying any of the newfangled psychological methods so much in vogue nowadays. There was nothing said about making the seats easy or the lessons easy. We were simply driven pointblank against our books like soldiers against the enemy, and sternly ordered, "Up and at 'em. Commit your lessons to memory!" If we failed in any part, however slight, we were whipped; for the grand, simple, all-sufficing Scotch discovery had been made that there was a close connection between the skin and the memory, and that irritating the skin excited the memory to any required degree.

With my school lessons father made me learn hymns and Bible verses. For learning "Rock of Ages" he gave me a penny, and I thus became suddenly rich. Scotch boys are seldom spoiled with money. We thought more of a penny those economical days than the poorest American schoolboy thinks of a dollar. To decide what to do with that first penny was an extravagantly serious affair. I ran in great excitement up and down the street, examining the tempting goodies in the shop windows before venturing on so important an investment. My playmates also became excited when the wonderful news got

Above: *A fall mist creates familiar and sweet solitude.* Opposite: *Oak leaves, Yosemite Valley.*

abroad that Johnnie Muir had a penny, hoping to obtain a taste of the orange, apple, or candy it was likely to bring forth.

Just before school skaled (closed), we all arose and sang the fine hymn "Lord, dismiss us with Thy blessing." In the spring when the swallows were coming back from their winter homes we sang —
Welcome, welcome, little stranger,
Welcome from a foreign shore:
Safe escaped from many a danger. . .
and while singing we all swayed in rhythm with the music. "The Cuckoo," that always told his name in the spring of the year, was another favorite song, and when there was nothing in particular to call to mind any special bird or animal, the songs we sang were widely varied, such as
The whale, the whale is the beast for me,
Plunging along through the deep, deep sea.
But the best of all was "Lord, dismiss us with Thy blessing," though at that time the most significant part I fear was the first three words.

I was so proud of my skill as a climber that when I first heard of hell from a servant girl who loved to tell its horrors and warn us that if we did anything wrong we would be cast into it, I always insisted that I could climb out of it. I imagined it was only a sooty pit with stone walls like those of the castle, and I felt sure there must be chinks and cracks in the masonry for fingers and toes. Anyhow the terrors of the horrible place seldom lasted long beyond the telling; for natural faith casts out fear.

[N]o punishment, however sure and severe, was of any avail against the attraction of the fields and woods. It had other uses, developing memory, etc., but in keeping us at home it was of no use at all. Wildness was ever sounding in our ears, and Nature saw to it that besides school lessons and church lessons some of her own lessons should be learned, perhaps with a view to the time when we should be called to wander in wildness to our heart's content. Oh, the blessed enchantment of those Saturday run-aways in the prime of the spring! How our young wondering eyes reveled in the sunny, breezy glory of the hills and the sky, every particle of us thrilling and tingling with the bees and glad birds and glad streams! Kings may be blessed; we were glorious, we were free—school

The wilderness air is sometimes sharp yet heavy with moisture that becomes hoarfrost.

cares and scoldings, heart thrashings and flesh thrashings alike, were forgotten in the fullness of Nature's glad wildness. These were my first excursions — the beginnings of lifelong wanderings.

[In 1849, when he was eleven years old, John Muir came with his father to America, and settled near Portage, Wisconsin. — Ed. Note]

This sudden plash into pure wildness—baptism in Nature's warm heart — how utterly happy it made us! Nature streaming into us, wooingly teaching her wonderful glowing lessons, so unlike the dismal grammar ashes and cinders so long thrashed into us. Here without knowing it we still were at school; every wild lesson a love lesson, not whipped but charmed into us. Oh, that glorious Wisconsin wilderness!

But those first days and weeks of unmixed enjoyment and freedom, reveling in the wonderful wildness about us, were soon to be mingled with the hard work of making a farm. I was first put to burning brush in clearing land for the plough. Those magnificent brush fires with great white hearts and red flames, the first big, wild outdoor fires I had ever seen, were wonderful sights for young eyes. Again and again, when they were burning fiercest so that we could hardly approach near enough to throw on another branch, father put them to awfully practical use as warning lessons, comparing their heat with that of hell, and the branches with bad boys. "Now, John," he would say, "now, John, just think what an awful thing it would be to be thrown into that fire — and then, think of hell-fire, that is so many times hotter. Into that fire all bad boys, with sinners of every sort who disobey God, will be cast as we are casting branches into this brush fire, and although suffering so much, their suffering will never, never end, because neither the fire nor the sinners can die." But those terrible fire lessons quickly faded away in the blithe wilderness air; for no fire can be hotter than the heavenly fire of faith and hope that burns in every healthy boy's heart.

A little church was established among the earlier settlers and the meetings at first were held in our house. After working hard all the week it was difficult for boys to sit still through long sermons without falling asleep, especially in warm weather. In this drowsy trouble the charming anemone came to our help. A pocketful of the pungent seeds industriously nibbled while the discourses were at their dullest kept us awake and filled our minds with flowers.

Many of our old neighbors toiled and sweated and grubbed themselves into their graves years before their natural dying days, in getting a living on a quarter-section of land and vaguely trying to get rich, while bread and raiment might have been serenely won on less than a fourth of this land, and time gained to get better acquainted with God.

In those early days, long before the great labor-saving machines came to our help, almost everything connected with wheat-raising abounded in trying work — cradling in the long, sweaty dog-days, raking and binding, stacking, thrashing — and it often seemed to me that our fierce, over-industrious way of getting the grain from the ground was too closely connected with grave-digging. The staff of life, naturally beautiful, oftentimes suggested the grave-digger's spade. Men and boys, and in those days even women and girls, were cut down while cutting the wheat. The fat folk grew lean and the lean leaner, while the rosy cheeks brought from Scotland and other cool countries across the sea faded to yellow like the wheat. We were all made slaves through the vice of over-industry. The same was in great part true in making hay to keep the cattle and horses through the long winters. We were called in the morning at four o'clock and seldom got to bed before nine, making a broiling, seething day seventeen hours long loaded with heavy work, while I was only a small stunted boy; and a few years later my brothers David and Daniel and my older sisters had to endure about as much as I did. In the

National Park Service

John Muir: "I wandered away on a glorious botanical and geological excursion, which has lasted nearly fifty years and is not yet completed, always happy and free. . . ."

harvest dog-days and dog-nights and dog-mornings, when we arose from our clammy beds, our cotton shirts clung to our backs as wet with sweat as the bathing-suits of swimmers, and remained so all the long, sweltering days. In mowing and cradling, the most exhausting of all the farm work, I made matters worse by foolish ambition in keeping ahead of the hired men. Never a warning word was spoken of the dangers of over-work. On the contrary, even when sick we were held to our tasks as long as we could stand. Once in harvest-time I had the mumps and was unable to swallow any food except milk, but this was not allowed to make any difference, while I staggered with weakness and sometimes fell headlong among the sheaves. Only once was I allowed to leave the harvest-field — when I was stricken with pneumonia. I lay gasping for weeks, but the Scotch are hard to kill and I pulled through. No physician was called, for father was an enthusiast, and always said and believed that God and hard work were by far the best doctors.

None of our neighbors were so excessively industrious as father; though nearly all of the Scotch, English, and Irish worked too hard, trying to make good homes and to lay up money enough for comfortable independence. Excepting small garden-patches, few of them had owned land in the old country. Here their craving land-hunger was satisfied, and they were naturally proud of their farms and tried to keep them as neat and clean and well-tilled as gardens. To accomplish this without the means for hiring help was impossible. Flowers were planted about the neatly kept log or frame houses; barnyards, granaries, etc., were kept in about as neat order as the homes, and the fences and corn-rows were rigidly straight. But every uncut weed distressed them; so also did every ungathered ear of grain, and all that was lost by birds and gophers; and this overcarefulness bred endless work and worry. . . .

The American settlers were wisely content with smaller fields and less of everything, kept indoors during excessively hot or cold weather, rested when tired, went off fishing and hunting at the most favorable times and seasons of the day and year, gathered nuts and berries, and in general tranquilly accepted all the good things the fertile wilderness offered.

[I]n the third or fourth of our Wisconsin winters there was a magnificently colored aurora that was seen and admired over nearly all the continent. The whole sky was draped in graceful purple and crimson folds glorious beyond description. Father called us out into the yard in front of the house where we had a wide view, crying: "Come! Come, mother! Come bairns! and see the glory of God. All the sky is clad in a robe of red light. Look straight up to the crown where the folds are gathered. Hush and wonder and adore, for surely this is the clothing of the Lord Himself, and perhaps He will even now appear looking down from His high heaven."

On Sundays, after or before chores and sermons and Bible-lessons, we drifted about on the lake for hours, especially in lily time, getting finest lessons and sermons from the water and flowers, ducks, fishes, and muskrats. In particular we took Christ's advice and devoutly "considered the lilies" — how they grow up in beauty out of gray lime mud, and ride gloriously among the breezy sun-spangles.

The warmth of the deep spring fountains of the creek in our meadow kept it open all the year, and a few pairs of wood ducks, the most beautiful, we thought, of all the ducks, wintered in it. I well remember the first specimen I ever saw. Father shot it in the creek during a snowstorm, brought it into the house, and called us around him, saying: "Come bairns, and admire the work of God displayed in this bonnie bird. Nobody but God could paint feathers like these."

The pup was a common cur, though very uncommon to us, a black and white short-haired mongrel that we named "Watch." We always gave him a pan of milk in the evening just before we knelt in family worship, while daylight still lingered in the shanty. And, instead of attending to the prayers, I too often studied the small wild creatures playing around us. Field mice scampered about the cabin as though it had been

built for them alone, and their performances were very amusing. About dusk, on one of the calm, sultry nights so grateful to moths and beetles, when the puppy was lapping his milk, and we were on our knees, in through the door came a heavy broad-shouldered beetle about as big as a mouse, and after it had droned and boomed round the cabin two or three times, the pan of milk, showing white in the gloaming, caught its eyes, and taking good aim, it alighted with a slanting, glinting plash in the middle of the pan like a duck alighting in a lake. Baby Watch, having never before seen anything like that beetle, started back, gazing in dumb astonishment and fear at the black sprawling monster trying to swim. Recovering somewhat from his fright, he began to bark at the creature, and ran round and round his milk-pan, wouf-woufing, gurring, growling, like an old dog barking at a wild-cat or a bear. The natural astonishment and curiosity of that boy dog getting his first entomological lesson in this wonderful world was so immoderately funny that I had great difficulty in keeping from laughing out loud. . . .

When he was about six or seven years old, he not only became cross, so that he would do only what he liked, but he fell on evil ways, and was accused by the neighbors who had settled around us of catching and devouring whole broods of chickens, some of them only a day or two out of the shell. We never imagined he would do anything so grossly undoglike. He never did at home. But several of the neighbors declared over and over again that they had caught him in the act, and insisted that he must be shot. At last, in spite of tearful protests, he was condemned and executed. Father examined the poor fellow's stomach in search of sure evidence, and discovered the heads of eight chickens that he had devoured at his last meal. So poor Watch was killed simply because his taste for chickens was too much like our own. Think of the millions of squabs that preaching, praying men and women kill and eat, with all sorts of other animals great and small, young and old, while eloquently discoursing on the coming of the blessed peaceful, bloodless millennium! Think of the passenger pigeons that fifty or sixty years

Kent and Donna Dannen

Top left and above: *"We drifted about the lake for hours, especially in lily time, getting finest lessons and sermons from the water and flowers, ducks, fishes, and muskrats."*

ago filled the woods and sky over half the continent, now exterminated by beating down the young from the nests together with the brooding parents, before they could try their wonderful wings; by trapping them in nets, feeding them to hogs, etc. None of our fellow mortals is safe who eats what we eat, who in any way interferes with our pleasures, or who may be used for work or food, clothing or ornament, or mere cruel, sportish amusement. Fortunately many are too small to be seen, and therefore enjoy life beyond our reach.

One of the gayest of the singers is the redwing blackbird. . . . In summer, after nesting cares are over, they assemble in flocks of hundreds and thousands to feast on Indian corn when it is in the mild. Scattering over a field, each selects an ear, strips the husk far enough to lay bare an inch or two of the end of it, enjoys an exhilarating feast, and after all are full they rise simultaneously with a quick birr of wings like an old-fashioned church congregation fluttering to their feet when the minister after giving out the hymn says, "Let the congregation arise and sing."

The love-songs of the frogs seemed hardly less wonderful than those of the birds, their musical notes varying from the sweet, tranquil, soothing peeping and purring of the hylas to the awfully deep low-bass blunt bellowing of the bullfrogs. Some of the smaller species have wonderfully clear, sharp voices and told us their good Bible names in musical tones about as plainly as the whip-poor-will. *Isaac, Isaac; Yacob, Yacob; Israel, Israel;* shouted in sharp, ringing, far-reaching tones, as if they had all been to school and severely drilled in elocution. In the still, warm evenings, big bunchy bullfrogs bellowed, *Drunk! Drunk! Drunk! Jug o' rum! Jug o' rum!* and early in the spring, countless thousands of the commonest species, up to the throat in cold water, sang in concert, making a mass of music, such as it was, loud enough to be heard at a distance of more than half a mile.

One of our July days was spent with two Scotch boys of our own age hunting redwing blackbirds then busy in the corn-fields. Our party had only one single-barreled shotgun, which, as the oldest and perhaps because I was thought to be the best shot, I had the honor of carrying. We marched through the corn without getting sight of a single redwing, but just as we reached the far side of the field, a redheaded woodpecker flew up, and the Lawson boys cried: "Shoot him! Shoot him! He is just as bad as a blackbird. He eats corn!" This memorable woodpecker alighted in the top of a white oak tree about fifty feet high. I fired from a position almost immediately beneath him, and he fell straight down at my feet. When I picked him up and was admiring his plumage, he moved his legs slightly, and I said, "Poor bird, he's no deed yet and we'll hae to kill him to put him oot o' pain" — sincerely pitying him, after we had taken pleasure in shooting him. I had seen servant girls wringing chicken necks, so with desperate humanity I took the limp unfortunate by the head, swung him around three or four times thinking I was wringing his neck, and then threw him hard on the ground to quench the last possible spark of life and make quick death doubly sure. But to our astonishment the moment he struck the ground he gave a cry of alarm and flew right straight up like a rejoicing lark into the top of the same tree, and perhaps to the same branch he had fallen from, and began to adjust his ruffled feathers, nodding and chirping and looking down at us as if wondering what in the bird world we had been doing to him. This of course banished all thought of killing, as far as that revived woodpecker was concerned, no matter how many ears of corn he might spoil, and we all heartily congratulated him on his wonderful, triumphant resurrection from three kinds of death — shooting, neck-wringing, and destructive concussion. I suppose only one pellet had touched him, glancing on his head.

Surely a better time must be drawing nigh when godlike human beings will become truly humane, and learn to put their animal fellow mortals in their hearts instead of on their backs or in their dinners. In the meantime we may just

*The silent woodpecker pecks and drills
into tree trunks and limbs for larvae and insects.
His staccato attacks reverberate throughout the forest.*

as well as not learn to live clean innocent lives instead of slimy, bloody ones. All hale, red-blooded boys are savage, the best and boldest the savagest, fond of hunting and fishing. But when thoughtless childhood is past, the best rise the highest above all this bloody flesh and sport business, the wild foundational animal dying out day by day, as divine uplifting, transfiguring charity grows in.

It was a great memorable day when the first flock of passenger pigeons came to our farm, calling to mind the story we had read about them when we were at school in Scotland. Of all God's feathered people that sailed the Wisconsin sky, no other bird seemed to us so wonderful.

And surely all God's people, however serious and savage, great or small, like to play. Whales and elephants, dancing, humming gnats, and invisibly small mischievous microbes — all are warm with divine radium and must have lots of fun in them.

The old Scotch fashion of whipping for every act of disobedience or of simple, playful forgetfulness was still kept up in the wilderness, and of course many of those whippings fell upon me. Most of them were outrageously severe, and utterly barren of fun. But here is one that was nearly all fun.

Father was busy hauling lumber for the frame house that was to be got ready for the arrival of my mother, sisters, and brother, left behind in Scotland. One morning, when he was ready to start for another load, his ox-whip was not to be found. He asked me if I knew anything about it. I told him I didn't know where it was, but Scotch conscience compelled me to confess that when I was playing with it I had tied it to Watch's tail, and that he ran away, dragging it through the grass, and came back without it. "It must have slipped off his tail," I said, and so I didn't know where it was. This honest, straightforward little story made father so angry that he exclaimed with heavy, forboding emphasis: "The very dee-vil's in that boy!" David, who had been playing with me and was perhaps about as responsible

for the loss of the whip as I was, said never a word, for he was always prudent enough hold his tongue when the parental weather was stormy, and so escaped nearly all punishment. And, strange to say, this time I also escaped, all except a terrible scolding, though the thrashing weather seemed darker than ever. As if unwilling to let the sun see the shameful job, father took me into the cabin where the storm was to fall, and sent David to the woods for a switch. While he was out selecting the switch, father put in the spare time sketching my play-wickedness in awful colors, and of course referred again and again to the place prepared for bad boys. In the midst of this terrible word-storm, dreading most

the impending thrashing, I whimpered that I was only playing because I couldn't help it; didn't know I was doing wrong; wouldn't do it again, and so forth. After this miserable dialogue was about exhausted, father became impatient at my brother for taking so long to find the switch; and so was I, for I wanted to have the thing over and done with. At last, in came David, a picture of open-hearted innocence, solemnly dragging a young bur-oak sapling, and handed the end of it to father, saying it was the best switch he could find. It was an awfully heavy one, about two and a half inches thick at the butt and ten feet long, almost big enough for a fence-pole. There wasn't room enough in the cabin to swing it, and the moment I saw it I burst out laughing in the midst of my fears. But father failed to see the fun and was very angry at David, heaved the bur-oak outside and passionately demanded his reason for fetching "sic a muckle rail like that instead o' a switch? Do ye ca' that a switch? I have a gude mind to thrash you insteed o' John." David, with demure, downcast eyes, looked preternaturally righteous, but as usual prudently answered never a word.

It was a hard job in those days to bring up Scotch boys in the way they should go; and poor overworked father was determined to do it if enough of the right kind of switches could be found. But this time, as the sun was getting high, he hitched up old Tom and Jerry and made haste to the Kingston lumber-yard, leaving me unscathed and as innocently wicked as ever; for hardly had father got fairly out of sight among the oaks and hickories, ere all our troubles, hell-threatenings, and exhortations were forgotten in the fun we had lassoing a stubborn old sow and laboriously trying to teach her to go reasonably steady in rope harness. She was the first hog that father bought to stock the farm, and we boys regarded her as a very wonderful beast. In a few weeks she had a lot of pigs, and of all the queer, funny, animal children we had yet seen, none amused us more. They were so comic in size and shape, in their gait and gestures, their merry sham fights, and the false alarms they got up for the fun of scampering back to their mother and begging her in most persuasive little squeals to lie down and give them a drink.

After her darling short-snouted babies were about a month old, she took them out to the woods and gradually roamed farther and farther from the shanty in search or acorns and roots. One afternoon we heard a rifle-shot, a very noticeable thing, as we had no near neighbors, as yet. We thought it must have been fired by an Indian on the trail that followed the right bank of the Fox River between Portage and Packwaukee Lake and passed our shanty at a distance of about three quarters of a mile. Just a few minutes after that shot was heard, along came the poor mother rushing up to the shanty for protection, with her pigs, all out of breath and terror-stricken. One of them was missing, and we supposed of course that an Indian had shot it for food. Next day, I discovered a blood-puddle where the Indian trail crossed the outlet of our lake. One of father's hired men told us that the Indians thought nothing of levying this sort of blackmail whenever they were hungry. The solemn awe and fear in the eyes of that old mother and those little pigs I never can forget; it was an unmistakable and deadly a fear as I ever saw expressed by any human eye, and corroborates in no uncertain way the oneness of all of us.

My father was a steadfast enthusiast on religious matters, and, of course, attended almost every sort of church-meeting, especially revival meetings. They were occasionally held in summer, but mostly in winter when the sleighing was good and plenty of time available. One hot summer day father drove Nob to Portage and back, twenty-four miles over a sandy road. It was a hot, hard, sultry day's work, and she had evidently been over-driven in order to get home in time for one of these meetings. I shall never forget how tired and wilted she looked that evening when I unhitched her; how she dropped in her stall, too tired to eat or even to lie down. Next morning it was plain that her lungs were inflamed; all the dreadful symptoms were just the same as my own when I had pneumonia. Father sent for a Methodist minister, a very energetic, resourceful man, who was a blacksmith, farmer, butcher, and horse-doctor as well as minister; but all his gifts and skill were of no avail. Nob was doomed. We bathed her head and tried to get her to eat something, but she couldn't eat, and in about a couple of weeks we turned her loose to let her come around the house and see us in the weary suffering and loneliness of the shadow of death. She tried to follow us children, so long her friends and workmates and playmates. It was awfully touching. She had several hemorrhages, and in the forenoon of her last day, after she had had one of her dreadful spells of bleeding and gasping for breath, she came to me trembling, with beseeching, heartbreaking looks, and after I had bathed her head and tried to soothe and pet her, she lay down and gasped and died. All the family gathered about her, weeping, with aching hearts. Then dust to dust.

She was the most faithful, intelligent, playful, affectionate, human-like horse I ever knew, and she won all our hearts. Of the many advantages of farm life for boys one of the greatest is the gaining a real knowledge of animals as fellow-mortals, learning to respect them and love them, and even to win some of their love. Thus godlike sympathy grows and thrives and spreads far beyond the teachings of churches and schools, where too often the mean, blinding, loveless doctrine is taught that animals have neither mind nor soul, have no rights that we are bound to respect, and were made only for man, to be petted, spoiled, slaughtered, or enslaved.

. . . I was fond of reading, but father had brought only a few religious books from Scotland. Fortunately, several of our neighbors had brought a dozen or two of all sorts of books, which I borrowed and read, keeping all of them except the religious ones carefully hidden from father's eye. Among these were Scott's novels, which like all other novels, were strictly forbidden, but devoured with glorious pleasure in secret. Father was easily persuaded to buy Josephus's *Wars of the Jews,* and D'Aubigné's *History of the Reformation,* and I tried hard to get him to buy *Plutarch's Lives,* which, as I told him, everybody, even religious people, praised as a grand good book; but he would have nothing to do with the old pagan until the graham bread and anti-flesh doctrines came suddenly into our backwoods neighborhood, making a stir something like phrenology and spirit-rappings, which were as mysterious in their attacks as influenza. He then thought it possible that Plutarch might be turned to account on the food question by revealing what those old Greeks and Romans ate to make them strong; and so at last we gained our glorious Plutarch. Dick's *Christian Philosopher,* which I borrowed from a neighbor, I thought I might venture to read in the open, trusting that the word "Christian" would be proof against its cautious condemna-

tion. But father balked at the word "Philosopher," and quoted from the Bible a verse which spoke of "philosophy falsely so-called." I then ventured to speak in defense of the book, arguing that we could not do without at least a little of the most useful kinds of philosophy.

"Yes, we can," he said with enthusiasm, "the Bible is the only book human beings can possibly require throughout all the journey from earth to heaven."

"But how," I contended, "can we find the way to heaven without the Bible, and how after we grow old can we read the Bible without a little helpful science? Just think, father, you cannot read your Bible without spectacles, and millions of others are in the same fix; and spectacles cannot be made without some knowledge of the science of optics."

"Oh!" he replied, perceiving the drift of the argument, "there will always be plenty of worldly people to make spectacles."

To this I stubbornly replied with a quotation from the Bible with reference to the time coming when "all shall know the Lord from the least even to the greatest," and then who will make the spectacles? But he still objected to my reading that book, called me a contumacious quibbler too fond of disputation, and ordered me to return it to the accommodating owner. I managed, however, to read it later.

On the food question father insisted that those who argued for a vegetable diet were in the right, because our teeth showed plainly that they were made with reference to fruit and grain and not for flesh like those of dogs and wolves and tigers. He therefore promptly adopted a vegetable diet and requested mother to make the bread from graham flour instead of bolted flour. Mother put both kinds on the table, and meat also, to let all the family take their choice, and while father was insisting on the foolishness of eating flesh, I came to her help by calling father's attention to the passage in the Bible which told the story of Elijah the prophet who, when he was pursued by enemies who wanted to take his life, was hidden by the Lord by the brook Cherith, and fed by ravens; and surely the Lord knew what was good to eat, whether bread

Working on a farm gave Muir the opportunity to know animals as fellow-mortals, worthy of respect and love.

or meat. And on what, I asked, did the Lord feed Elijah? On vegetables or graham bread? No, he directed the ravens to feed his prophet on flesh. The Bible being the sole rule, father at once acknowledged that he was mistaken. The Lord never would have sent flesh to Elijah by the ravens if graham bread were better.

I remember as a great and sudden discovery that the poetry of the Bible, Shakespeare, and Milton was a source of inspiring, exhilarating, uplifting pleasure; and I became anxious to know all the poets, and saved up small sums to buy as many of their books as possible. Within three or four years I was the proud possessor of parts of Shakespeare's, Milton's, Cowper's, Henry Kirke White's, Campbell's, and Akenside's works, and quite a number of others seldom read nowadays. I think it was in my fifteenth year that I began to relish good literature with enthusiasm, and smack my lips over favorite lines, but there was desperately little time for reading, even in the winter evenings — only a few stolen minutes now and then. Father's strict rule was, straight to bed immediately after family worship, which in winter was usually over by eight o'clock. I was in the habit of lingering in the kitchen with a book and candle after the rest of the family had retired, and considered myself fortunate if I got five minutes' reading before father noticed the light and ordered me to bed; an order that of course I immediately obeyed. But night after night I tried to steal minutes in the same lingering way, and how keenly precious those minutes were, few nowadays can

know. Father failed perhaps two or three times in a whole winter to notice my light for nearly ten minutes, magnificent golden blocks of time, long to be remembered like holidays or geological periods. One evening when I was reading Church history father was particularly irritable, and called out with hope-killing emphasis, *"John, go to bed!* Must I give you a separate order every night to get you to go to bed? Now, I will have no irregularity in the family; you *must* go when the rest go, and without my having to tell you." Then, as an afterthought, as if judging that his words and tone of voice were too severe for so pardonable an offense as reading a religious book, he unwarily added: "If you *will* read, get up in the morning and read. You may get up in the morning as early as you like."

That night I went to bed wishing with all my heart and soul that somebody or something might call me out of sleep to avail myself of this wonderful indulgence; and next morning to my joyful surprise I awoke before father called me. A boy sleeps soundly after working all day in the snowy woods, but that frosty morning I sprang out of bed as if called by a trumpet blast, rushed downstairs, scarce feeling my chilblains,

enormously eager to see how much time I had won; and when I held up my candle to a little clock that stood on a bracket in the kitchen I found that it was only one o'clock. I had gained five hours, almost half a day! "Five hours to myself!" I said, "five huge, solid hours!" I can hardly think of any other event in my life, any discovery I ever made that gave birth to joy so transportingly glorious as the possession of these five frosty hours.

. . . [T]o enter the State University . . . was my ambition, and it never wavered no matter what I was doing. No University, it seemed to me, could be more admirably situated, and as I sauntered about it, charmed with its fine lawns and trees and beautiful lakes, and saw the students going and coming with their books, and occasionally practicing with a theodolite in measuring distances, I thought that if I could only join them it would be the greatest joy of life. I was desperately hungry and thirsty for knowledge and willing to endure anything to get it.

One day I chanced to meet a student who had noticed my inventions at the Fair and now recognized me. And when I said, "You are

Learning was Muir's way of life, whether reading in the quiet of the night (opposite) or studying the veined blooms of the moccasin flower (right).

Kent and Donna Dannen

fortunate fellows to be allowed to study in this beautiful place. I wish I could join you." "Well, why don't you?" he asked. "I haven't money enough," I said. "Oh, as to money," he reassuringly explained, "very little is required. I presume you're able to enter the Freshman class, and you can board yourself as quite a number of us do at a cost of about a dollar a week. The baker and milkman come every day. You can live on bread and milk." Well, I thought, maybe I have money enough for at least one beginning term. Anyhow I couldn't help trying.

With fear and trembling, overladen with ignorance, I called on Professor Stirling, the Dean of the Faculty, who was then Acting President, presented my case, and told him how far I had got on with my studies at home, and that I hadn't been to school since leaving Scotland at the age of eleven years, excepting one short term of a couple of months at a district school, because I could not be spared from the farm work. After hearing my story, the kind professor welcomed me to the glorious University — next, it seemed to me, to the Kingdom of Heaven.

I received my first lesson in botany from a student by the name of Griswold, who is now County Judge of the County of Waukesha, Wisconsin. In the University he was often laughed at on account of his anxiety to instruct others, and his frequently saying with fine emphasis, "Imparting instruction is my greatest enjoyment." One memorable day in June, when I was standing on the stone steps of the north dormitory, Mr. Griswold joined me and at once began to teach. He reached up, plucked a flower from an overspreading branch of a locust tree, and, handing it to me, said, "Muir, do you know what family this tree belongs to?"

"No," I said, "I don't know anything about botany."

"Well, no matter," said he, "what is it like?"

"It's like a pea flower," I replied.

"That's right. You're right," he said, "it belongs to the Pea Family."

"But how can that be," I objected, "when the pea is a weak, clinging, straggling herb, and the locust a big, thorny hardwood tree?"

"Yes, that is true," he replied, "as to the difference in size, but it is also true that in all their essential characters they are alike, and therefore they must belong to one and the same family. Just look at the peculiar form of the locust flower; you see the upper petal, called the banner, is broad and erect, and so is the upper petal of the pea flower; the two lower petals, called the wings, are outspread and wing-shaped; so are those of the pea; and the two petals below the wings are united on their edges, curve upward, and form what is called the keel, and so you see are the corresponding petals of the pea flower. And now look at the stamens and pistils. You see that nine of the ten stamens have their filaments united into a sheath around the pistil, but the tenth stamen has its filament free. These are very marked characters, are they not? And, strange to say, you will find them the same in the tree and in the vine. Now look at the ovules or seeds of the locust, and you will see that they are arranged in a pod or legume like those of the pea. And look at the leaves. You see the leaf of the locust is made up of several leaflets, and so also is the leaf of the pea. Now taste the locust leaf."

I did so and found that it tasted like the leaf of the pea. Nature has used the same seasoning for both, though one is a straggling vine, the other a big tree.

"Now, surely you cannot imagine that all these similar characters are mere coincidences. Do they not rather go to show that the Creator in making pea vine and locust tree had the same idea in mind, and that plants are not classified arbitrarily? Man has nothing to do with their classification. Nature has attended to all that, giving essential unity with boundless variety, so that the botanist has only to examine plants to learn the harmony of their relations."

This fine lesson charmed me and sent me flying to the woods and meadows in wild enthusiasm. Like everybody else I was always fond of flowers, attracted by their external beauty and purity. Now my eyes were opened to their inner beauty, all alike revealing glorious traces of the thoughts of God, and leading on and on into the infinite cosmos. I wandered away at every opportunity, making long excursions round the lakes, gathering specimens and keeping them fresh in a bucket in my room to study at night after my regular class tasks were learned; for

my eyes never closed on the plant glory I had seen.

Although I was four years at the University, I did not take the regular course of studies, but instead picked out what I thought would be most useful to me, particularly chemistry, which opened a new world, and mathematics and physics, a little Greek and Latin, botany and geology. I was far from satisfied with what I had learned, and should have stayed longer. Anyhow I wandered away on a glorious botanical and geological excursion, which has lasted nearly

fifty years and is not yet completed, always happy and free, poor and rich, without thought of a diploma or of making a name, urged on and on through endless, inspiring, godful beauty.

From the top of a hill on the north side of Lake Mendota I gained a last wistful, lingering view of the beautiful University grounds and buildings where I had spent so many hungry and happy and hopeful days. There with streaming eyes I bade my blessed Alma Mater farewell. But I was only leaving one University for another, the Wisconsin University for the University of the Wilderness.

Fog patterned on coastal hills, Monterey Peninsula, California: "Endless, inspiring, godful beauty."

The Forests
of America

John Muir was at home in the forest. Woodlands gave him his boyhood experiences with wilderness, and botany always was his first love among the natural sciences. His consuming interest in the various types of trees took him on several excursions through the forests of Eastern America during his early adult years. The last and longest of these was a thousand-mile walk from Indiana to the Gulf of Mexico. After a side-trip to see Cuban forests, Muir then set sail for California, land of the big trees, which was to be his new home.

But to Muir trees were not only objects of study. Forests were places of worship for all living things. The trees themselves were a "worshiping multitude." Individual trees or particular species were priests who led the worship and gave instruction on holy matters.

Trees were not human, but they were "people." That is, they were individuals with their own personalities and their own value in the eyes of God. Like men, and with more understanding than men, trees participated in the loving activity of God in Nature.

If Muir never quite convinced America that trees were worshiping "people," he did convince many Americans that their forests held great spiritual riches as well as material riches. If trees themselves did not reach up to God, they at least made it possible for man to do so. This was more than sufficient reason to preserve them in the purity of wilderness.

Opposite: *Snow-brushed giants, Sequoia National Park, California.*

32

Opposite: *"Going to the woods is going home. . . ."* Above: *To Muir, trees were not only objects of study, they were places of worship for all living things.* Overleaf: *In the wilderness one sometimes seems to be in a majestic domed pavilion.*

The forests of America, however slighted by man, must have been a great delight to God; for they were the best he ever planted.

Our National Parks

Going to the woods is going home. . . .

Our National Parks

The air is distinctly fragrant with balsam and resin and mint — every breath of it a gift we may well thank God for. Who could ever guess that so rough a wilderness should yet be so fine, so full of good things. One seems to be in a majestic domed pavilion in which a grand play is being acted with scenery and music and incense — all the furniture and action so interesting we are in no danger of being called on to endure one dull moment. God himself seems to be always doing his best here, working like a man in a glow of enthusiasm.

My First Summer in the Sierra

[T]o learn how they [trees] live and behave in pure wildness, to see them in their varying aspects through the seasons and weather, rejoicing in the great storms, in the spiritual mountain light, putting forth their new leaves and flowers when all the streams are in flood and the birds are singing, and sending away their seeds in the thoughtful Indian summer when all the landscape is glowing in deep calm enthusiasm — for this you must love them and live with them, as free from schemes and cares and time as the trees themselves.

Our National Parks

As twilight began to fall, I sat down on the mossy instep of a spruce. Not a bush or tree was moving; every leaf seemed hushed in brooding repose. One bird, a thrush, embroidered the silence with cheery notes, making the solitude familiar and sweet, while the solemn monotone of the stream sifting through the woods seemed like the very voice of God, humanized, terrestrialized, and entering one's heart as to a home prepared for it. Go where we will, all the world over, we seem to have been there before.

Travels in Alaska

They tell us that plants are perishable, soulless creatures, that only man is immortal, etc.; but this I think is something that we know very nearly nothing about. Anyhow, this palm was indescribably impressive and told me grander things than I ever got from human priest.

A Thousand-Mile Walk to the Gulf

These forests were composed of about five hundred species of trees, all of them in some way useful to man, ranging in size from twenty-five feet in height and less than one foot in diameter at the ground to four hundred feet in height and more than twenty feet in diameter — lordly monarchs proclaiming the gospel of beauty like apostles.

Our National Parks

When one is alone at night in the depths of these woods, the stillness is at once awful and sublime. Every leaf seems to speak. One gets close to Nature, and the love of beauty grows as it cannot in the distractions of a camp. . . . Jubilant winds and waters sound in grand harmonious symphonies — wild music flowing on forever from a thousand thousand sources, winds in hollows of the glaciers glinting on crystal angles, winds on crags, in trees, among the elastic needles sweeping soft and low with silken rhythm, and winds murmuring through the grasses, ring the bells of Bryanthus.

Journal entry on Mt. Ranier

Every tree during the progress of gentle storms is loaded with fairy bloom at the coldest and darkest time of year, bending the branches, and hushing every singing needle.

The Mountains of California

God's glacial mills grind slowly, but they have been kept in motion long enough in California to grind sufficient soil for a glorious abundance of life, though most of the grist has been carried to the lowlands, leaving these high regions comparatively lean and bare; while the post-glacial agents of erosion have not yet furnished sufficient available food over the general surface for more than a few tufts of the hardiest plants, chiefly carices and eriogonae. And it is interesting to learn in this connection that the sparseness and repressed character of the vegetation at this height is caused more by want of soil than by harshness of climate; for, here and there, in sheltered hollows (counter-sunk beneath the general surface) into which a few rods of well-ground moraine chips have been dumped, we find groves of spruce and pine thirty to forty feet high, trimmed around the edges with willow and huckleberry bushes, and oftentimes still further by an outer ring of tall grasses, bright with lupines, larkspurs, and showy columbines, suggesting a climate by no means repressingly severe. All the streams, too, and the pools at this elevation are furnished with little gardens wherever soil can be made to lie, which, though making scarce any show at a distance, constitute charming surprises to the appreciative observer. In these bits of leafiness a few birds find grateful homes. Having no acquaintance with man, they fear no ill, and flock curiously about the stranger, almost allowing themselves to be taken in the hand. In so wild and so beautiful a region was spent my first day, every sight and sound inspiring, leading one far out of himself, yet feeding and building up his individuality.

The Mountains of California

I'm beneath that grand old pine that I have heard so often in storms both at night and in the day. It sings grandly now, every needle sun-thrilled and shining and responding tunefully to the azure wind. . . .

In the evening Black and I rode together up into the sugar pine forests and on to his old ranch in the moonlight. The grand priest-like pines held their arms above us in blessing. The wind sang songs of welcome. The cool glaciers and the running crystal fountains were in it. I was no longer *on* but *in* the mountains — home again, and my pulses were filled. On and on in white moonlight-spangles on the streams, shadows in rock hollows and briery ravines, tree architecture on the sky more divine than ever stars in their spires, leafy mosaic in meadow and bank. Never had the Sierra seemed so inexhaustible — mile on mile onward in the forest through groves old and young, pine tassles overarching and brushing both cheeks at once. The chirping of crickets only deepened the stillness. . . .

Miles and miles of tree scripture along the sky, a bible that will one day be read! The beauty of its letters and sentences have burned me like fire through all these Sierra seasons. Yet I cannot interpret their hidden thoughts. They are terrestrial expressions of the sun, pure as water and snow. Heavens! listen to the wind song! I'm still writing beneath that grand old pine in Black's yard and that other companion, scarcely less noble, back of which I sheltered during the earthquake, is just a few yards beyond. The shadows of their boles lie like charred logs on the gray, while half the yard is embroidered with their branches and leaves. There goes a woodpecker with an acorn to drive into its thick bark for winter, and well it may gather its stores, for I can myself detect winter in the wind.

Few nights of my mountain life have been more eventful than that of my ride in the woods from Coulterville, where I made my reunion with the winds and pines. It was eleven o'clock when we reached Black's ranch. I was weary and soon died in sleep. How cool and vital and recreative was the hale young mountain air. On higher, higher into the holy of holies of the woods! Pure white lustrous clouds overshadowed the massive congregations of silver fir and pine. We entered, and a thousand living arms were waved in

Yosemite Valley and Merced River from valley floor.

solemn blessing. An infinity of mountain life. How complete is the absorption of one's life into the spirit of mountain woods. No one can love or hate an enemy here, for no one can conceive of such a creature as an enemy. Nor can one have any distinctive love of friends. The dearest and best of you all seemed of no special account, mere trifles. . . .

Along the Merced divide to the ancient glacial lake-bowl of Crane's Flat, was ever fir or pine more perfect? What groves! What combinations of green and silver gray and glowing white of glinting sunbeams. Where is leaf or limb awanting, and is this the upshot of the so-called "mountain glooms" and mountain storms? If so, is Sierra forestry aught beside an outflow of Divine Love? . . . [I]t is just where these crushing glaciers have born down most heavily that the grandest loveliness of grove and forest appears.

Letter to Mrs. Ezra S. Carr
from Yosemite Valley

Only spread a fern frond over a man's head and worldly cares are cast out, and freedom and beauty and peace come in. . . . It would seem impossible that any one, however incrusted with care, could escape the godful influence of these sacred forests. Yet this very day I saw a shepherd pass through one of the finest of them without betraying more feeling than his sheep. "What do you think of these grand ferns?" I asked. "Oh, they're only d--d big brakes," he replied.

My First Summer in the Sierra

Oftentimes I had to sleep out without blankets, and also without supper or breakfast. But usually I had no great difficulty in finding a loaf of bread in the widely scattered clearings of the farmers. With one of these big backwoods loaves I was able to wander many a long mile, free as the winds in the glorious forests and bogs, gathering plants and feeding on God's abounding, inexhaustible spiritual beauty bread.

A Thousand-Mile Walk to the Gulf

I miss my river songs tonight. Here Hazel Creek at its topmost springs has a voice like a

A study in textures: ferns near the base of a ponderosa pine.

bird. The wind-tones in the great trees overhead are strangely impressive, all the more because not a leaf stirs below them. But it grows late, and I must to bed. The camp is silent; everybody asleep. It seems extravagant to spend hours so precious in sleep. "He giveth his beloved sleep." Pity the poor beloved needs it, weak, weary, forspent; oh, the pity of it, to sleep in the midst of eternal, beautiful motion instead of gazing forever, like the stars.

My First Summer in the Sierra

...The rain brought out the colors of the woods with delightful freshness, the rich brown of the bark of the trees and the fallen burs and leaves and dead ferns; the grays of rocks and lichens; the light purple of swelling buds, and the warm yellow greens of the libocedrus and mosses. The air was steaming with delightful fragrance, not rising and wafting past in separate masses, but diffused through all the atmosphere. Pine woods are always fragrant, but most so in spring when the young tassels are opening and in warm weather when the various gums and balsams are softened by the sun. The wind was now chafing their innumerable needles and the

warm rain was steeping them. Monardella grows here in large beds in the openings, and there is plenty of laurel in dells and manzanita on the hillsides, and the rosy, fragrant chamoebatia carpets the ground almost everywhere. These, with the gums and balsams of the woods, form the main local fragrance-fountains of the storm.

The Mountains of California

...Then the rain began to abate and I sauntered down through the dripping bushes reveling in the universal vigor and freshness that inspired all the life about me. How clean and unworn and immortal the woods seemed to be! — the lofty cedars in full bloom laden with golden pollen and their washed plumes shining; the pines rocking gently and settling back into rest, and the evening sunbeams spangling on the broad leaves of the madroños, their tracery of yellow boughs relieved against dusky thickets of chestnut oak; liverworts, lycopodiums, ferns were exulting in glorious revival, and every moss that had ever lived seemed to be coming crowding back from the dead to clothe each trunk and stone in living green. The steaming ground seemed fairly to throb and tingle with

Tenaya Lake, Sierra Nevada: "The solemn monotone of the stream sifting through the woods. . . ."

life; smilax, fritillaria, saxifrage, and young violets were pushing up as if already conscious of the summer glory, and innumerable green and yellow buds were peeping and smiling everywhere.

The Mountains of California

[F]ew indeed, strong and free with eyes undimmed with care, have gone far enough and lived long enough with the trees to gain anything like a loving conception of their grandeur and significance as manifested in the harmonies of their distribution and varying aspects throughout the seasons, as they stand arrayed in their winter garb rejoicing in storms, putting forth their fresh leaves in the spring while steaming with resiny fragrance, receiving the thundershowers of summer, or reposing heavy-laden with ripe cones in the rich sun-gold of autumn. For knowledge of this kind one must dwell with the trees and grow with them, without any reference to time in the almanac sense.

The Mountains of California

On the mossy trunk of an old prostrate spruce about a hundred feet in length thousands of

seedlings were growing. I counted seven hundred on a length of eight feet, so favorable is this climate for the development of tree seeds and so fully do these trees obey the command to multiply and replenish the earth.

Travels in Alaska

Vines growing on roadsides receive many a tormenting blow, simply because they give evidence of feeling. Sensitive people are served in the same way. But the roadside vine soon becomes less sensitive, like people getting used to teasing — Nature, in this instance, making for the comfort of flower creatures the same benevolent arrangement as for man. Thus I found that the *Schrankia* vines growing along footpaths leading to a backwoods schoolhouse were much less sensitive than those in the adjacent unfrequented woods, having learned to pay but slight attention to the tingling strokes they get from teasing scholars.

A Thousand-Mile Walk to the Gulf

There is always something deeply exciting, not only in the sounds of winds in the woods, which exert more or less influence over every

Left: *Yellow-throated gilia, found in high meadows.*
Opposite: *Redbud tree in Kings Canyon, Sierra: Few
have lived long enough with trees to gain a loving
conception of their grandeur throughout the seasons.*

mind, but in their varied water-like flow as
manifested by the movements of the trees,
especially those of the conifers. By no other
trees are they rendered so extensively and
impressively visible, not even by the lordly
tropic palms or tree-ferns responsive to the
gentlest breeze. The waving of a forest of the
giant sequoias is indescribably impressive and
sublime, but the pines seem to me the best
interpreters of winds. They are mighty waving
goldenrods, ever in tune, singing and writing
wind-music all their long century lives.

The Mountains of California

I found most of the trees here fairly loaded
with mosses. Some broadly palmated branches
had beds of yellow moss so wide and deep that
when wet they must weigh a hundred pounds or
even more. Upon these moss-beds ferns and
grasses and even goodsized seedling trees grow,
making beautiful hanging gardens in which the
curious spectacle is presented of old trees holding hundreds of their own children in their arms,
nourished by rain and dew and the decaying
leaves showered down to them by their parents.

Travels in Alaska

[O]ur big fire, heaped high with resiny logs and
branches, is blazing like a sunrise, gladly giving
back the light slowly sifted from the sunbeams of
centuries of summers; and in the glow of that old
sunlight how impressively surrounding objects
are brought forward in relief against the outer
darkness! Grasses, larkspurs, columbines, lilies,
hazel bushes, and the great trees form a circle
around the fire like thoughtful spectators, gazing
and listening with human-like enthusiasm.

My First Summer in the Sierra

I walked from Louisville a distance of one
hundred and seventy miles, and my feet are
sore. But, oh! I am paid for all my toil a thousand
times over. I am in the woods on a hilltop with
my back against a moss-clad log. I wish you
could see my last evening's bedroom. The sun
has been among the tree-tops for more than an
hour; the dew is nearly all taken back, and the
shade in these hill basins is creeping away
into the unbroken strongholds of the grand
old forests.

I have enjoyed the trees and scenery of Kentucky exceedingly. How shall I ever tell of the
miles and miles of beauty that have been flowing
into me in such measure? These lofty curving
ranks of ... hills, these concealed valleys of
fathomless verdure, and these lordly trees with
the nursing sunlight glancing in their leaves
upon the outlines of the magnificent masses of
shade embosomed among their wide branches —
these are cut into my memory to go with me
forever.

A Thousand-Mile Walk to the Gulf

Far the grandest of all Kentucky plants are
her noble oaks. They are the master existences
of her exuberant forests. Here is the Eden, the
paradise of oaks.

A Thousand-Mile Walk to the Gulf

After we were fairly out of the bay into Ste-
phens Passage, the wind died away, and the
Indians had to take to their oars again, which
ended our talk. On we sped over the silvery
level, close alongshore. The dark forests extending far and near, planted like a field of wheat,
might seem monotonous in the general views,
but the appreciative observer, looking closely,
will find no lack of interesting variety, however
far he may go. The steep slopes on which they
grow allow almost every individual tree, with its
particularities of form and color, to be seen like
an audience on seats rising above one another —

(continued on p. 45)

Opposite: *Moss-covered sequoias and pines, Mariposa Grove, Yosemite.* Right: *Muir loved to wander, free as the winds, gathering plants in the glorious forests.*

the blue-green, sharply-tapered spires of the Menzies spruce, the warm yellow-green Mertens spruce with their finger-like tops all pointing in the same direction, or drooping gracefully like leaves of grass, and the airy, feathery, brownish-green Alaska cedar. The outer fringe of bushes along the shore and hanging over the brows of the cliffs, the white mountains above, the shining water beneath, the changing sky over all, form pictures of divine beauty in which no healthy eye may ever grow weary.

Travels in Alaska

The coniferous forests of the Sierra are the grandest and most beautiful in the world. . . .

The Mountains of California

. . .The coniferous woods of Canada, and the Carolinas, and Florida, are made up of trees that resemble one another about as nearly as blades of grass, and grow close together in much the same way. Coniferous trees, in general, seldom possess individual character, such as is manifest among oaks and elms. But the California forests are made up of a greater number of distinct species than any other in the world. And in them we find, not only a marked differentiation into special groups, but also a marked individuality in almost every tree, giving rise to storm effects indescribably glorious.

The Mountains of California

Right gladly we pushed our way into the wild untrampled kingdoms of the Sierra, inspired with the thousand indefinite joys of the green summer woods. . . .

San Francisco Daily Evening Bulletin
August 13, 1875

This is a dear bonnie morning, the sun rays lovingly to His precious pines. The brown meadows are nightly frosted browner and the yellow aspens are losing their leaves. I wish I could write to you, but hard work near and far presses heavily and I cannot. Nature makes huge demands, yet pays a thousand, thousand fold. As in all the mountains I have seen about the head of the Merced and Tuolumne this region is a song of God. . . .

Letter to Mrs. Ezra S. Carr
from the South Fork of the San Joaquin River

Sauntering up the foothills to . . . Yosemite Park, richer and wilder become the forests and streams. At an elevation of six thousand feet above the level of the sea the silver firs are two hundred feet high, with branches whorled around the colossal shafts in regular order, and every branch beautifully pinnate like a fern frond. The Douglas spruce, the yellow and sugar pines and brown-barked libocedrus here reach their finest developments of beauty and grandeur. The majestic sequoia is here, too, the king of conifers, the noblest of all the noble race. These colossal trees are as wonderful in fineness of beauty and proportion as in stature — an assemblage of conifers surpassing all that have ever yet been discovered in the forests of the world. Here, indeed, is the tree-lover's paradise; the woods, dry and wholesome, letting in the light in shimmering masses of half sunshine, half shade; the night air as well as the day air indescribably spicy and exhilarating. . . .

The Yosemite

The giant pines, and firs, and sequoias hold their arms open to the sunlight, rising above one

Kent and Donna Dannen

another on the mountain benches, marshaled in glorious array, giving forth the utmost expression of grandeur and beauty with inexhaustible variety and harmony.

The Mountains of California

[A]bout two hours after beginning the descent, we found ourselves among the sugar pine groves at the lower end of the valley, through which we rode in perfect ecstasy, for never did pines seem so noble and religious in all their gestures and tones. The sun pouring down mellow gold, seemed to be shining only for them, and the wind gave them voice, but the gestures of their outstretched arms appeared wholly independent of the winds, and impressed one with a solemn awe that overbore all our knowledge of causes and brought us into the condition of beings new-arrived from some other far-off world. The ground was smoothly strewn with dead, clean leaves and burs, making a fine brown surface for shadows, many a wide even bar, from tapering trunk columns, and rich mosaic from living leaf and branch. There amid the groves we came to small openings without a tree or shadow, wholly filled with the sun, like pools of glowing light. . . .

Our ride up the valley was perfectly enchanting, every bend of the river presenting reaches of surpassing loveliness, sunbeams streaming through its border groves, or falling in broad masses upon the white rapids or calm, deep pools. Here and there a dead pine that had been swept down in flood time reached out over the current, its green mosses and lichens contrasting with the crystal sheen of the water, and its gnarled roots forming shadowy caves for speckled trout where the current eddies slowly, and protecting sedges and willows dip their leaves. Among these varied and ever-changing river reaches the appreciative artist may find studies for a lifetime.

San Francisco Daily Evening Bulletin
August 13, 1875

No lover of trees will ever forget his first meeting with the sugar pine, nor will he afterward need a poet to call him to "listen what the pine tree saith." In most pine trees there is a sameness of expression, which, to most people, is apt to become monotonous; for the typical spiry form, however beautiful, affords but little scope for appreciable individual character. The sugar pine is as free from conventionalities of form and motion as any oak. No two are alike, even to the most inattentive observer; and, notwithstanding they are ever tossing out their immense arms in what might seem most extravagant gestures, there is a majesty and repose about them that precludes all possibility of the grotesque, or even picturesque, in their general expression. They are the priests of pines, and seem ever to be addressing the surrounding forest. . . .

No other pine seems to me so unfamiliar and self-contained. In approaching it, we feel as if in

The merry, continually chattering squirrel (opposite) adds insouciant note to the wilderness, contrasting with somber moods evoked by the redwood forest (right).

David Muench

the presence of a superior being, and begin to walk with a light step, holding our breath. Then, perchance, while we gaze awe-stricken, along comes a merry squirrel, chattering and laughing, to break the spell, running up the trunk with no ceremony, and gnawing off the cones as if they were made only for him; while the carpenter woodpecker hammers away at the bark, drilling holes in which to store his winter supply of acorns.

Although so wild and unconventional when full-grown, the sugar pine is a remarkably proper tree in youth. The old is the most original and independent in appearance of all the Sierra evergreens; the young is the most regular — a strict follower of coniferous fashions — slim, erect, with leafy, supple branches kept exactly in place, each tapering in outline and terminating in a spiry point. The successive transitional forms presented between the cautious neatness of youth and bold freedom of maturity offer a delightful study. At the age of fifty or sixty years, the shy, fashionable form begins to be broken up. Specialized branches push out in the most unthought-of places, and bend with the great cones, at once marking individual character, and this being constantly augmented from year to year by the varying action of the sunlight, winds, snowstorms, etc., the individuality of the tree is never again lost in the general forest.

The Mountains of California

Unfortunately, the sugar pine makes excellent lumber. It is too good to live, and is already passing rapidly away before the woodman's axe. Surely out of all the abounding forest-wealth of Oregon a few specimens might be spared to the world, not as dead lumber, but as living trees. A park of moderate extent might be set apart and protected for public use forever, containing at least a few hundreds of each of these noble pines, spruces, and firs. Happy will be the men who, having the power and the love and benevolent forecast to do this, will do it. They will not be forgotten. The trees and their lovers will sing their praises, and generations yet unborn will rise up and call them blessed.

Steep Trails

Were they [ponderosa pine] mere mechanical sculptures, what noble objects they would still be! How much more throbbing, thrilling, overflowing, full of life in every fibre and cell, grand glowing silver-rods — the very gods of the plant kingdom, living their sublime century lives in sight of Heaven, watched and loved and admired from generation to generation! . . . How rich our inheritance in these blessed mountains, the tree pastures into which our eyes are turned!

My First Summer in the Sierra

The most influential of the Valley trees is the yellow pine (*Pinus ponderosa*). . . . Climbing these grand trees, especially when they are waving and singing in worship in wind storms, is a glorious experience. Ascending from the lowest branch to the topmost is like stepping up stairs through a blaze of white light, every needle thrilling and shining as if with religious ecstasy.

The Yosemite

While exploring the forest zones of Mount Shasta, I discovered the path of a hurricane strewn with thousands of pines of this species. Great and small had been uprooted or wrenched off by sheer force, making a clean gap, like that made by a snow avalanche. But hurricanes capable of doing this class of work are rare in the Sierra, and when we have explored the forests from one extremity of the range to the other, we are compelled to believe that they are the most beautiful on the face of the earth.

The Mountains of California

Walk in the sequoia woods at any time of the year and you will say they are the most beautiful and majestic on earth.

The Mountains of California

[I]t is not easy to account for the colossal size of the sequoias. The largest are about three hundred feet high, and thirty feet in diameter. Who of all the dwellers of the plains and prairies and fertile home forests of roundheaded oak and maple, hickory and elm, ever dreamed that earth could bear such growths? — trees that the familiar pines and firs seem to know nothing about, lonely, silent, serene, with a physiognomy almost godlike, and so old, thousands of them still living had already counted their years by tens of centuries when Columbus set sail from Spain, and were in the vigor of youth or middle age when the star led the Chaldean sages to the infant Savior's cradle. As far as man is concerned, they are the same yesterday, today, and forever, emblems of permanence.

No description can give any adequate idea of their singular majesty, much less of their beauty....Only in youth does it show, like other conifers, a heavenward yearning, keenly aspiring with a long quick-growing top. Indeed the whole tree, for the first century or two, or until a hundred to a hundred and fifty feet high, is arrowhead in form, and, compared with the solemn rigidity of age, is as sensitive to the wind as a squirrel's tail. The lower branches are gradually dropped as it grows older, and the upper ones thinned out, until comparatively few are left. These, however, are developed to a great size, divide again and again, and terminate in bossy rounded masses of leafy branchlets, while the head is dome-shaped. Then poised in fullness of strength and beauty, stern and solemn in mien, it glows with eager, enthusiastic life, quivering to the tip of every leaf and branch and far-reaching root, calm as a granite dome — the first to feel the touch of the rosy beams of the morning, the last to bid the sun good night.

...It is a curious fact that all the very old sequoias have lost their heads by lightning. "All things come to him who waits;" but of all living things Sequoia is perhaps the only one able to wait long enough to make sure of being struck by lightning. Thousands of years it stands ready and waiting, offering its head to every passing cloud as if inviting its fate, praying for heaven's fire as a blessing; and when at last the old head is off, another of the same shape immediately begins to grow on. Every bud and branch seems excited, like bees that have lost their queen, and tries hard to repair the damage. Branches that for many centuries have been growing out horizontally at once turn upward, and all their branchlets arrange themselves with reference to a new top of the same peculiar curve as the old one. Even the small subordinate branches halfway down the trunk do their best to push up to the top and help in this curious head-making.

"Hunting Big Redwoods," *The Atlantic Monthly* September 1901

But though so consummately beautiful, the Big Tree always seems unfamiliar, with peculiar physiognomy, awfully solemn and earnest; yet with all its strangeness it impresses us as being more at home than any of its neighbors, holding the best right to the ground as the oldest, strongest inhabitant. One soon becomes acquainted with new species of pine and fir and

spruce as with friendly people, shaking their outstretched branches like shaking hands and fondling their little ones, while the venerable aboriginal sequoia, ancient of other days, keeps you at a distance, looking as strange in aspect and behavior among its neighbor trees as would the mastodon among the homely bears and deer.

The Yosemite

So far as I am able to see at present only fire and the ax threaten the existence of those noblest of God's trees. In Nature's keeping they are safe, but through the agency of man, destruction is making rapid progress, while in the work of protection only a good beginning has been made.

The Yosemite

[T]he finest block of Big Tree forest in the entire belt is on the north fork of Tule River. In the northern groves there are comparatively few young trees or saplings. But here for every old,

storm-stricken giant there are many in all the glory of prime vigor, and for each of these a crowd of eager, hopeful young trees and saplings growing heartily on moraines, rocky ledges, along watercourses, and in the moist alluvium of meadows, seemingly in hot pursuit of eternal life. . . .

I never saw a Big Tree that had died a natural death; barring accidents they seem to be immortal, being exempt from all the diseases that afflict and kill other trees. Unless destroyed by man, they live on indefinitely until burned, smashed by lightning, or cast down by storms, or by the giving way of the ground on which they stand. . . .No other tree in the world . . . opens such impressive and suggestive views into history. . . .

The Mountains of California

We heard the sound of axes, and soon came upon a group of busy men engaged in preparing a butt section of a giant sequoia they had felled for exhibition at the Quaker Centennial. ... Many a poor, defrauded town dweller will pay his dollar and peep, and gain some dead arithmetical notion of the bigness of our Big Trees, but a true and living knowledge of these tree gods is not to be had at so cheap a rate. As well try to send a section of the storms on which they feed.

San Francisco Daily Evening Bulletin
August 13, 1875

In studying the fate of our forest king, we have thus far considered the action of purely natural causes only; but, unfortunately, *man* is in the woods, and waste and pure destruction are making rapid headway. If the importance of forests were at all understood, even from an economic standpoint, their preservation would call forth the most watchful attention of government. Only of late years by means of forest reservations has the simplest groundwork for available legislation been laid, while in many of the finest groves every species of destruction is still moving on with accelerated speed.

It appears, therefore, that notwithstanding our forest king might live on gloriously in Nature's keeping, it is rapidly vanishing before the fire and steel of man; and unless protective measures be speedily invented and applied, in a few decades, at the farthest, all that will be left of *Sequoia gigantea* will be a few hacked and scarred monuments.

The Mountains of California

We are often told that the world is going from bad to worse, sacrificing everything to mammon. But this righteous uprising in defense of God's trees in the midst of exciting politics and wars is telling a different story, and every sequoia, I fancy, has heard the good news and is waving its branches for joy. The wrongs done to trees, wrongs of every sort, are done in the darkness of ignorance and unbelief, for when light comes the heart of the people is always right. Forty-seven years ago one of these Calaveras King Sequoias was laboriously cut down, that the stump might be had for a dancing floor. Another, one of the

finest in the grove, more than three hundred feet high, was skinned alive to a height of one hundred and sixteen feet from the ground and the bark sent to London to show how fine and big that Calaveras tree was — as sensible a scheme as skinning our great men would be to prove their greatness. This grand tree is of course dead, a ghastly disfigured ruin, but it still stands erect and holds forth its majestic arms as if alive and saying, "Forgive them; they know not what they do." Now some millmen want to cut all the Calaveras trees into lumber and money. But we have found a better use for them. No doubt these trees would make good lumber after passing through a sawmill, as George Washington after passing through the hands of a French cook would have made good food. But both for Washington and the tree that bears his name higher uses have been found.

Could one of these sequoia kings come to town in all its godlike majesty so as to be strikingly seen and allowed to plead its own cause, there would never again by any lack of defenders. And the same may be said of all the other sequoia groves and forests of the Sierra with their companions and the noble *Sequoia sempervirens,* or redwood, of the coast mountains.

Sierra Club Bulletin
January 1920

Both of the silver firs [white fir and California red fir] live between two and three centuries when the conditions about them are at all favorable. Some venerable patriarch may be seen heavily storm-marked, towering in severe majesty above the rising generations, with a protecting grove of hopeful saplings pressing close around his feet, each dressed with such loving care that not a leaf seems wanting.

The Yosemite

A dry spot a little way back from the margin of a silver fir lily-garden makes a glorious campground, especially where the slope is toward the east with a view of the distant peaks along the summit of the range. The tall lilies are brought forward most impressively like visitors by the light of your campfire and the nearest of the

trees with their whorled branches tower above you like larger lilies and the sky seen through the garden-opening seems one vast meadow of white lily stars.

The Yosemite

Every tree-lover is sure to regard it [Western hemlock] with special admiration; apathetic mountaineers, even, seeking only game or gold, stop to gaze on first meeting it, and mutter to themselves: "That's a mighty pretty tree," some of them adding, "d–d pretty!"

The Mountains of California

[A]t a height of about 11,000 feet you find patches of the tough, whitebarked pine, pressed so flat by the ten or twenty feet of snow piled upon them every winter for centuries that you may walk over them as if walking on a shaggy rug. And, if curious about such things, you may discover specimens of this hardy tree-mountaineer not more than four feet high and about as many inches in diameter at the ground, that are from two hundred to four hundred years old, still holding bravely to life, making the most of their slender summers, shaking their tasseled needles in the breeze right cheerily, drinking the thin sunshine and maturing their fine purple cones as if they meant to live forever.

The Yosemite

The juniper or red cedar *(Juniperus occidentalis)* is preeminently a rock tree, occupying the baldest domes and pavements in the upper silver fir and alpine zones, at a height of from 7,000 to 9,500 feet. . . .It never makes anything like a forest; seldom even a grove. Usually it stands out separate and independent, clinging by slight joints to the rocks, living chiefly on snow and thin air and maintaining sound health on this diet for 2,000 years or more. Every feature or every gesture it makes expresses steadfast, dogged endurance. . . .

Barring accidents, for all I can see they would live forever; even when overthrown by avalanches, they refuse to lie at rest, lean stubbornly on their big branches as if anxious to rise, and while a single root holds to the rock, put forth fresh leaves with a grim, never-say-die expression.

The Yosemite

. . .a sturdy storm-enduring mountaineer of a tree. . . .

The Mountains of California

Wish I could live, like these junipers, on sunshine and snow, and stand beside them on the shore of Lake Tenaya for a thousand years. How much I should see, and how delightful it would be! Everything in the mountains would find me and come to me, and everything from the heavens like light.

My First Summer in the Sierra

[Western white pine] is the noblest tree of the alpine zone — hardy and long-lived, towering grandly above its companions and becoming stronger and more imposing just where other species begin to crouch and disappear. . . . [I]t begins to show its distinguishing characteristic in the most marked way at an elevation of about 10,000 feet, extending its tough, rather slender arms in the frosty air, welcoming the storms and feeding on them and reaching sometimes the grand old age of 1,000 years.

The Yosemite

All the larger streams of uncultivated countries are mysteriously charming and beautiful, whether flowing in mountains or through swamps and plains. Their channels are interestingly sculptured, far more so than the grandest architectural works of man. The finest of the forests are usually found along their banks, and in the multitude of falls and rapids in the wilderness finds a voice. Such a river is the Hiwassee, with its surface broken to a thousand sparkling gems, and its forest walls vine-draped and flowery as Eden. And how fine the songs it sings!

A Thousand-Mile Walk to the Gulf

The glowing sunset beams fall in bars through the forest, touching with marvelous power the hushed waiting firs, yellow ferns, and glistening

grass stems that grow in sandy moraines, and the aster and goldenrods along our camp meadow. . . .

Two large bucks with branched antlers like dead pine roots are splendidly framed in willows as they stand in grasses over their backs — noble inhabitants of this wild forest.

Journal entry on the Middle Fork
of the San Joaquin River

The Douglas squirrel is by far the most interesting and influential of the California sciuridae, surpassing every other species in force of character, numbers, and extent of range, and in the amount of influence he brings to bear upon the health and distribution of the vast forests he inhabits. . . .

I cannot begin to tell here how much he has cheered my lonely wanderings during all the years I have been pursuing my studies in these glorious wilds; or how much unmistakable humanity I have found in him. Take this for example: One calm, creamy Indian summer morning, when the nuts were ripe, I was camped in the upper pine woods of the south fork of the San Joaquin, where the squirrels seemed to be about as plentiful as the ripe burs. They were taking an early breakfast before going to their regular harvest work. While I was busy with my own breakfast, I heard the thudding fall of two or three heavy cones from a yellow pine near me. I stole noiselessly forward within about twenty feet of the base of it to observe. In a few

moments down came the Douglas. The breakfast burs he had cut off had rolled on the gently sloping ground into a clump of ceanothus bushes, but he seemed to know exactly where they were, for he found them at once, apparently without searching for them. They were more than twice as heavy as himself, but after turning them into the right position for getting a good hold with his long sickle-teeth he managed to drag them up to the foot of the tree from which he had cut them, moving backward. Then seating himself comfortably, he held them on end, bottom up, and demolished them at his ease. A good deal of nibbling had to be done before he got anything to eat, because the lower scales are barren, but when he had patiently worked his way up to the fertile ones he found two sweet nuts at the base of each, shaped like trimmed hams, and spotted purple like birds' eggs. And notwithstanding these cones were dripping with soft balsam, and covered with prickles, and so strongly put together that a boy would be puzzled to cut them open with a jacknife, he accomplished his meal with easy dignity and cleanliness, making less effort apparently than a man would in eating soft cookery from a plate.

Breakfast done, I whistled a tune for him before he went to work, curious to see how he would be affected by it. He had not seen me all this while; but the instant I began to whistle he darted up the tree nearest to him, and came out on a small dead limb opposite me, and composed himself to listen. I sang and whistled more than

a dozen airs, and as the music changed his eyes sparkled, and he turned his head quickly from side to side, but made no other response. Other squirrels, hearing the strange sounds, came around on all sides, also chipmunks and birds. One of the birds, a handsome, speckled-breasted thrush, seemed even more interested than the squirrels. After listening for awhile on one of the lower dead sprays of a pine, he came swooping forward within a few feet of my face, and remained fluttering in the air for half a minute or so, sustaining himself with whirring wing-beats, like a hummingbird in front of a flower, while I could look into his eyes and see his innocent wonder.

By this time my performance must have lasted nearly half an hour. I sang or whistled "Bonnie Doon," "Lass o' Gowrie," "O'er the Water to Charlie," "Bonnie Woods o' Cragie Lee," etc., all of which seemed to be listened to with bright interest, my first Douglas sitting patiently through it all, with his telling eyes fixed upon me until I ventured to give the "Old Hundredth," when he screamed his Indian name, Pillillooeet, turned tail, and darted with ludicrous haste up the tree out of sight, his voice and actions in the case leaving a somewhat profane impression, as if he had said, "I'll be hanged if you get me to hear anything so solemn and unpiny." This acted as a signal for the general dispersal of the whole hairy tribe, though the birds seemed willing to wait further developments, music being naturally more in their line.

What there can be in that grand old church tune that is so offensive to birds and squirrels I can't imagine.

The Mountains of California

The Steller's jays were, of course, making more noise and stir than all the other birds combined; every coming and going with loud bluster, screaming as if each had a lump of melting sludge in his throat, and taking good care to improve every opportunity afforded by the darkness and confusion of the storm to steal from the acorn stores of the woodpeckers.

The Yosemite

As one strolls in the woods about the logging-camps, most of the lumbermen are found to be interesting people to meet, kind and obliging and sincere, full of knowledge concerning the bark and sapwood and heartwood of the trees they cut, and how to fell them without unnecessary breakage, on ground where they may be most advantageously sawed into logs and loaded for removal. The work is hard, and all of the older men have a tired, somewhat haggard appearance. Their faces are doubtful in color, neither sickly nor quite healthy-looking, and seamed with deep wrinkles like the bark of the spruces, but with no trace of anxiety. Their clothing is full of resin and never wears out. A little of everything in the woods is stuck fast to these loggers, and their trousers grow con-

Opposite, top: *Geology is written in layers of sediment.*
Above: *Steller's jays love to make noise and steal acorns from other birds.*

stantly thicker with age. In all their movements and gestures they are heavy and deliberate like the trees above them, and they walk with a swaying, rocking gait altogether free from quick, jerky fussiness, for chopping and log-rolling have quenched all that. They are also slow of speech, as if partly out of breath, and when one tries to draw them out on some subject away from logs, all the fresh, leafy, outreaching branches of the mind seem to have been withered and killed with fatigue, leaving their lives little more than dry lumber. Many a tree have these old axemen felled, but, round-shouldered and stooping, they too are beginning to lean over. Many of their companions are already beneath the moss, and among those that we see at work some are now dead at the top (bald), leafless, so to speak, and tottering to their fall.

A very different man, seen now and then at long intervals but usually invisible, is the free roamer of the wilderness — hunter, prospector, explorer, seeking he knows not what. Lithe and sinewy, he walks erect, making his way with the skill of wild animals, all his senses in action, watchful and alert, looking keenly at everything in sight, his imagination well nourished in the wealth of the wilderness, coming into contact with free nature in a thousand forms, drinking at the fountains of things, responsive to wild influences, as trees to the winds. Well he knows the wild animals his neighbors, what fishes are in the streams, what birds in the forests, and where food may be found. Hungry at times and weary, he has corresponding enjoyment in eating and resting, and all the wilderness is home.

Steep Trails

A New Sense
of Earth's Beauty

To John Muir, God's love was the central message of all nature. Earthquakes, storms, floods, as well as delicate flowers or birds' songs were expressions of love.

Death itself was merely a transition point when beauty changed its form. A snowflake melting to form a mirror lake was essentially the same as a doe dying and nourishing a wild orchid. This orderly procession in nature from one form of beauty to another demonstrated God's love for his world.

In 1867, four years after leaving the University of Wisconsin without a degree, Muir made a walking trip from Indiana to the Gulf of Mexico to study plant and animal life. In his extensive journals of the trip, published after his death, he wrote of the several days that he camped in the Bonaventure graveyard at Savannah, Georgia. There he was impressed by the contrast between the gloomy attitude toward death held by most men and the natural beauty of the cemetery. The plants and birds preached to Muir the good news of a harmony between life and death, of the interdependence among *all* aspects of nature. (Thus, he understood the basic principle of ecology before the word was invented and nearly a century before it became popular.)

The naturalist believed that men were unaware of nature's harmony either because the harmony was too complex for them to understand or because their understanding had been corrupted. Alienated from nature or lacking understanding, men feared death and were blind and deaf to the Creator's message of love. John Muir devoted his entire life to bringing awareness of this gospel of love to America.

Opposite: "*Wilderness so godful, cosmic, primeval bestows a new sense of earth's beauty and size.*"

Wilderness so godful, cosmic, primeval bestows a new sense of earth's beauty and size.
Steep Trails

The shocks and outbursts of earthquakes, volcanoes, geysers, storms, the pounding of waves, the uprush of sap in plants, each and all tell the orderly love-beats of Nature's heart.
Our National Parks

Nature is ever at work building and pulling down, creating and destroying, keeping everything whirling and flowing, allowing no rest but in rhythmical motion, chasing everything in endless song out of one beautiful form into another.
Our National Parks

[T]his destruction was creation, progress in the march of beauty through death.
Our National Parks

Some have strange morbid fears as soon as they find themselves with Nature, even in the kindest and wildest of her solitudes, like very sick children afraid of their mother — as if God were dead and the devil were king.
Steep Trails

The common robin, with all his familiar notes and gestures, is found nearly everywhere throughout the Park. . . .In all America he is at home, flying from plains to mountains, up and down, north and south, away and back, with the seasons and supply of food. Oftentimes in the High Sierra, as you wander through the solemn woods, awe-stricken and silent, you will hear the reassuring voice of this fellow wanderer ringing out sweet and clear as if saying, "Fear not, fear not. Only love is here."
Our National Parks

An inspiration is this song of the blessed lark, and universally absorbable by human souls. It seems to be the only bird-song of these hills that has been created with any direct reference to us. Music is one of the attributes of matter, into whatever forms it may be organized. Drops and sprays of air are specialized, and made to plash and churn in the bosom of a lark, as infinitesimal portions of air plash and sing about the angles and hollows of sand-grains, as perfectly composed and predestined as the rejoicing anthems of worlds; but our senses are not fine enough to catch the tones. Fancy the waving, pulsing melody of the vast flower-congregations of the Hollow flowing from myriad voices of tuned petal and pistil, and heaps of sculptured pollen. Scarce one note is for us; nevertheless, God be thanked for this blessed instrument hid beneath the feathers of a lark.
A Thousand-Mile Walk to the Gulf

The ouzel of all birds dares to enter a white torrent . . . not fearing to follow them through the darkest gorges, and coldest snow tunnels; acquainted with every waterfall, echoing their divine music; and throughout the whole of their beautiful lives interpreting all that we in our unbelief call terrible in the utterances of torrents, as only varied expressions of God's eternal love.
The Mountains of California

When at length we enter the mountain gateway, the somber rocks seem aware of our presence, and seem to come thronging closer about us. Happily the ouzel and the old familiar robin are here to sing us welcome, and azure daisies beam with trustfulness and sympathy, enabling us to feel something of Nature's love even here, beneath the gaze of her coldest rocks.
The Mountains of California

Never shall I forget these glad cascade songs, the low booming, the roaring, the keen, silvery clashing of the cool water rushing exulting from form to form beneath irised spray; or in the deep still night seen white in the darkness, and its multitude of voices sounding still more impressively sublime. Here I find the little water ouzel as much at home as any linnet in a leafy grove, seeming to take the greater delight the more boisterous the stream. The dizzy precipices, the swift dashing energy displayed, and the tender tones of the sheer falls are awe inspiring, but

Kent and Donna Dannen

The robin, Muir's "fellow wanderer," is at home in all America, including Sequoia National Park, above.

Muir was very fond of the "singularly joyous and lovable" water ouzel that flies underwater.

there is nothing awful about this little bird. Its song is sweet and low, and all its gestures, as it flits about amid the loud uproar, bespeak strength and peace and joy. Contemplating these darlings of Nature coming forth from spray-sprinkled nests on the brink of savage streams, Samson's riddle comes to mind, "Out of the strong cometh forth sweetness." A yet finer bloom is this little bird than the foam-bells in eddying pools. Gentle bird, a precious message you bring me. We may miss the meaning of the torrent, but thy sweet voice, only love is in it.

My First Summer in the Sierra

...Here, too, in this so-called "land of desolation," I met cassiope, growing in fringes among the battered rocks. Her blossoms had faded long ago, but they were still clinging with happy memories to the evergreen sprays, and still so beautiful as to thrill every fiber of one's being. Winter and summer, you may hear her voice, the low, sweet melody of her purple bells. No evangel among all the mountain plants speaks Nature's love more plainly than cassiope. Where she dwells, the redemption of the coldest solitude is complete. The very rocks and glaciers seem to feel her presence, and become imbued with her own fountain sweetness. All things were warming and awakening. Frozen rills began to

flow, the marmots came out of their nests in boulder piles and climbed sunny rocks to bask, and the dun-headed sparrows were flitting about seeking their breakfasts. The lakes seen from every ridge-top were brilliantly rippled and spangled, shimmering like the thickets of the low dwarf pines. The rocks, too, seemed responsive to the vital heat — rock crystals and snow crystals thrilling alike. I strode on exhilarated, as if never more to feel fatigue, limbs moving of themselves, every sense unfolding like the thawing flowers, to take part in the new day harmony.

The Mountains of California

July 2 — Warm, sunny day, thrilling plant and animals and rocks alike, making sap and blood flow fast, and making every particle of the crystal mountains throb and swirl and dance in glad accord like star-dust. No dullness anywhere visible or thinkable. No stagnation, no death. Everything kept in joyful rhythmic motion in the pulses of Nature's big heart.

My First Summer in the Sierra

When a page is written over but once it may be easily read; but if it be written over and over with characters of every size and style, it soon becomes unreadable, although not a single con-

Above: *Mt. Conness in upper left and Tenaya Lake, Sierra Nevada, capture the essence of high-country wilderness.* Opposite: *"The snow on the high mountains is melting fast and the streams are singing."*

fused meaningless mark or thought may occur among all the written characters. . . . Our limited powers are similarly perplexed and over-taxed in reading the inexhaustible pages of nature, for they are written over and over uncountable times, written in characters of every size and color, sentences composed of sentences, every part of a character a sentence. There is not a fragment in all nature, for every relative fragment of one thing is a full harmonious unit in itself. All together form the one grand palimpsest of the world.

A Thousand-Mile Walk to the Gulf

Nature is not so poor as to have only one of anything.

The Yosemite

The snow on the high mountains is melting fast, and the streams are singing bankfull, swaying softly through the level meadows and bogs, quivering with sun-spangles, swirling in pot-holes, resting in deep pools, leaping, shouting in wild, exulting energy over rough boulder dams, joyful, beautiful in all their forms. No Sierra landscape that I have seen holds anything truly dead or dull, or any trace of what in manufactories is called rubbish or waste; everything is perfectly clean and pure and full of divine lessons. This quick, inevitable interest attaching to everything seems marvelous until the hand of God becomes visible; then it seems reasonable that what interests Him may well interest us. When we try to pick out anything by itself, we find it hitched to everything else in the

(continued on p. 64)

Autumn in Sierra Nevada: "Nature is ever at work."

Calm before the storm in Utah's Uinta Mountains.

David Muench

universe. One fancies a heart like our own must be beating in every crystal and cell, and we feel like stopping to speak to the plants and animals as friendly fellow-mountaineers. Nature as a poet, an enthusiastic workingman, becomes more and more visible the farther and higher we go; for the mountains are fountains — beginning places, however related to sources beyond mortal ken.

My First Summer in the Sierra

September 9 — Weariness rested away and I feel eager and ready for another excursion a month or two long in the same wonderful wilderness. Now, however, I must turn toward the lowlands, praying and hoping Heaven will shove me back again.

The most telling thing learned in these mountain excursions is the influence of cleavage joints on the features sculptured from the general mass of the range. . . .Comprehended in general views, the features of the wildest landscape seem to be as harmoniously related as the features of a human face. Indeed, they look human and radiate spiritual beauty, divine thought, however covered and concealed by rock and snow.

My First Summer in the Sierra

Reading these grand mountain manuscripts displayed through every vicissitude of heat and cold, calm and storm, upheaving volcanoes and down-grinding glaciers, we see that everything in Nature called destruction must be creation — a change from beauty to beauty.

My First Summer in the Sierra

. . .One is constantly reminded of the infinite lavishness and fertility of Nature — inexhaustible abundance amid what seems enormous waste. And yet when we look into any of her operations that lie within reach of our minds, we learn that no particle of her material is wasted or worn out. It is eternally flowing from use to use, beauty to yet higher beauty; and we soon cease to lament waste and death, and rather rejoice and exult in the imperishable, unspendable wealth of the universe, and faithfully watch and wait the reappearance of everything that melts and fades and dies about us, feeling sure that its next appearance will be better and more beautiful than the last.

My First Summer in the Sierra

Thus, by forces seemingly antagonistic and destructive, has Mother Nature accomplished her beneficent designs — now a flood of fire, now a flood of ice, now a flood of water; and at length an outburst of organic life, a milky way of snowy petals and wings, girdling the rugged mountain like a cloud, as if the vivifying sunbeams beating against its sides had broken into a foam of plant bloom and bees, as sea waves break and bloom on a rock shore.

The Mountains of California

October 9 — After going again to the express office and post office, and wandering about the streets, I found a road which led me to the Bonaventure graveyard. If that burying-ground across the Sea of Galilee, mentioned in Scripture, was half as beautiful as Bonaventure, I do not wonder that a man should dwell among the

Kent and Donna Dannen

Bonaventure Cemetery, near Savannah, Georgia, has live oaks a century old (opposite) and graves (left) surrounded by magnolias and rose bushes.

tombs. It is only three or four miles from Savannah, and is reached by a smooth white shell road.

There is but little to be seen on the way in land, water, or sky, that would lead one to hope for the glories of Bonaventure. The ragged desolate fields, on both sides of the road, are overrun with coarse rank weeds, and show scarce a trace of cultivation. But soon all is changed. Rickety log huts, broken fences, and the last patch of weedy rice-stubble are left behind. You come to beds of purple liatris and living wild-wood trees. You hear the song of birds, cross a small stream, and are with Nature in the grand old forest graveyard, so beautiful that almost any sensible person would choose to dwell here with the dead rather than with the lazy, disorderly living.

Part of the grounds was cultivated and planted with live-oak, about a hundred years ago, by a wealthy gentleman who had his country residence here. But much the greater part is undisturbed. Even those spots which are disordered by art, Nature is ever at work to reclaim, and to make them look as if the foot of man had never known them. Only a small plot of ground is occupied with graves and the old mansion is in ruins. . . .

I gazed awe-stricken as one new-arrived from another world. Bonaventure is called a graveyard, a town of the dead, but the few graves are powerless in such a depth of life. The rippling of living waters, the song of birds, the joyous confidence of flowers, the calm, undisturbable

grandeur of the oaks, mark this place of graves as one of the Lord's most favored abodes of life and light.

On no subject are our ideas more warped and pitiable than on death. Instead of the sympathy, the friendly union, of life and death so apparent in Nature, we are taught that death is an accident, a deplorable punishment for the oldest sin, the arch-enemy of life, etc. Town children, especially, are steeped in this death orthodoxy, for the natural beauties of death are seldom seen or taught in towns.

Of death among our own species, to say nothing of the thousand styles and modes of murder, our best memories, even among happy deaths, yield groans and tears, mingled with morbid exultation; burial companies, black in cloth and countenance; and, last of all, a black box burial in an ill-omened place, haunted by imaginary glooms and ghosts of every degree. Thus death becomes fearful, and the most notable and incredible thing heard around a death-bed is, "I fear not to die."

But let children walk with Nature, let them see the beautiful blendings and communions of death and life, their joyous inseparable unity, as taught in woods and meadows, plains and mountains and streams of our blessed star, and they will learn that death is stingless indeed, and as beautiful as life, and that the grave has no victory, for it never fights. All is divine harmony.

Most of the few graves of Bonaventure are planted with flowers. There is generally a magnolia at the head, near the strictly erect marble,

a rose-bush or two at the foot, and some violets and showy exotics along the sides or on the tops. All is enclosed by a black iron railing, composed of rigid bars that might have been spears or bludgeons from a battlefield in Pandemonium.

It is interesting to observe how assiduously Nature seeks to remedy these labored art blunders. She corrodes the iron and marble, and gradually levels the hill which is always heaped up, as if a sufficiently heavy quantity of clods could not be laid on the dead. Arching grasses come one by one; seeds come flying on downy wings, silent as fate, to give life's dearest beauty for the ashes of art; and strong evergreen arms laden with ferns and tillandsia drapery are spread over all — Life at work everywhere, obliterating all memory of the confusion of man.

In Georgia many graves are covered with a common shingle roof, supported on four posts as the cover of a well, as if rain and sunshine were not regarded as blessings. Perhaps, in this hot and insalubrious climate, moisture and sunheat are considered necessary evils to which they do not wish to expose their dead.

The money package that I was expecting did not arrive until the following week. After stopping the first night at the cheap, disreputable-looking hotel, I had only about a dollar and a half left in my purse, and so was compelled to camp out to make it last in buying only bread. I went out of the noisy town to seek a sleeping place that was not marshy. After gaining the outskirts of town toward the sea, I found some low sand dunes, yellow with flowering solidagoes.

I wandered wearily from dune to dune sinking ankle-deep in the sand, searching for a place to sleep beneath the tall flowers, free from insects and snakes, and above all from my fellow man. But idle negroes were prowling about everywhere, and I was afraid. The wind had strange sounds, waving the heavy panicles over my head, and I feared sickness from malaria so prevalent here, when I suddenly thought of the graveyard.

"There," thought I, "is an ideal place for a penniless wanderer. There no superstitious prowling mischief maker dares venture for fear of haunting ghosts, while for me there will be God's rest and peace. And then, if I am to be exposed to unhealthy vapors, I shall have capi-

David Muench

"The moonlight sifted in auroral rays,
broidering the blackness in silvery light."

All the avenue where I walked was in shadow, but an exposed tombstone frequently shone out in startling whiteness on either hand, and thickets of sparkleberry bushes gleamed like heaps of crystals. Not a breath of air moved the gray moss, and the great black arms of the trees met overhead and covered the avenue. But the canopy was fissured by many a netted seam and leafy-edged opening, through which the moonlight sifted in auroral rays, broidering the blackness in silvery light. Though tired, I sauntered a while enchanted, then lay down under one of the great oaks. I found a little mound that served for a pillow, placed my plant press and bag beside me and rested fairly well, though somewhat disturbed by large prickly-footed beetles creeping across my hands and face, and by a lot of hungry stinging mosquitoes.

When I awoke, the sun was up and all Nature was rejoicing. Some birds had discovered me as an intruder, and were making a great ado in interesting language and gestures. I heard the screaming of the bald eagles, and of some strange waders in the rushes. I heard the hum of Savannah with the long jarring hallos of negroes far away. On rising I found that my head had been resting on a grave, and though my sleep had not been quite so sound as that of the person below, I arose refreshed, and looking about me, the morning sunbeams pouring through the oaks and gardens dripping with dew, the beauty displayed was so glorious and exhilarating that hunger and care seemed only a dream.

Eating a breakfast cracker or two and watching for a few hours the beautiful light, birds, squirrels, and insects, I returned to Savannah, to find that my money package had not yet arrived. I then decided to go early to the graveyard and make a nest with a roof to keep off the dew, as there was no way of finding out how long I might have to stay. I chose a hidden spot in a dense thicket of sparkleberry bushes, near the right bank of the Savannah River, where the bald eagles and a multitude of singing birds roosted. I was so well hidden that I had to carefully fix its compass bearing in my mind from a mark I made on the side of the main avenue, that I might be able to find it at bedtime.

tal compensation in seeing those grand oaks in the moon light, with all the impressive and nameless influences of this lonely beautiful place."

By this time it was near sunset, and I hastened across the common to the road and set off for Bonaventure, delighted with my choice, and almost glad to find that necessity had furnished me with so good an excuse for doing what I knew my mother would censure; for she made me promise I would not lie out of doors if I could possibly avoid it. The sun was set ere I was past the negroes' huts and rice fields, and I arrived near the graves in the silent hour of the gloaming.

I was very thirsty after walking so long in the muggy heat, a distance of three or four miles from the city, to get to this graveyard. A dull, sluggish, coffee-colored stream flows under the road just outside the graveyard garden park, from which I managed to get a drink after breaking a way down to the water through a dense fringe of bushes, daring the snakes and alligators in the dark. Thus refreshed I entered the weird and beautiful abode of the dead.

I used four of the bushes as corner posts for my little hut, which was about four or five feet long by about three or four in width, tied little branches across from forks in the bushes to support a roof of rushes, and spread a thick mattress of Long Moss over the floor for a bed. My whole establishment was on so small a scale that I could have taken up, not only my bed, but my whole house, and walked. There I lay that night, eating a few crackers.

Next day I returned to the town and was disappointed as usual in obtaining money. So after spending the day looking at the plants in the gardens of the fine residences and town squares, I returned to my graveyard home. That I might not be observed and suspected of hiding, as if I had committed a crime, I always went home after dark, and one night, as I lay down in my moss nest, I felt some cold-blooded creature in it; whether a snake or simply a frog or toad I do not know, but instinctively, instead of drawing back my hand, I grasped the poor creature and threw it over the tops of the bushes. That was the only significant disturbance or fright that I got.

"Camping Among the Tombs"
A Thousand-Mile Walk to the Gulf

In Yosemite Valley, one morning about two o'clock, I was aroused by an earthquake; and though I had never before enjoyed a storm of this sort, the strange, wild thrilling motion and rumbling could not be mistaken, and I ran out of my cabin, near the Sentinel Rock, both glad and frightened, shouting, "A noble earthquake!" feeling sure I was going to learn something. The shocks were so violent and varied, and succeeded one another so closely, one had to balance in walking as if on the deck of a ship among the waves, and it seemed impossible the high cliffs should escape being shattered. In particular, I feared that the sheer-fronted Sentinel Rock, which rises to a height of three thousand feet, would be shaken down, and I took shelter back of a big pine, hoping I might be protected from outbounding boulders, should any come so far. I was now convinced that an earthquake had been the maker of the taluses, and positive proof

soon came. It was a calm moonlight night, and no sound was heard for the first minute or two save a low muffled underground rumbling and a slight rustling of the agitated trees, as if, in wrestling with the mountains, Nature were holding her breath. Then, suddenly, out of the strange silence and strange motion there came a tremendous roar. The Eagle Rock, a short distance up the valley, had given way, and I saw it falling in thousands of the great boulders I had been studying so long, pouring to the valley floor in a free curve luminous from friction, making a terribly sublime and beautiful spectacle — an arc of fire fifteen hundred feet span, as true in form and as steady as a rainbow, in the midst of the stupendous roaring rock storm. The sound was inconceivably deep and broad and earnest, as if the whole earth, like a living creature, had at last found a voice and were calling to her sister planets. It seemed to me that if all the thunder I ever heard were condensed into one roar it would not equal this rock roar at the birth of a mountain talus. Think, then, of the roar that arose to heaven when all the thousands of ancient cañon taluses throughout the length and breadth of the range were simultaneously given birth.

The main storm was soon over, and, eager to see the new-born talus, I ran up the valley in the moonlight and climbed it before the huge blocks, after their wild fiery flight, had come to complete rest. They were slowly settling into their places, chafing, grating against one another, groaning, and whispering; but no motion was visible except in a stream of small fragments pattering down the face of the cliff at the head of the talus. A cloud of dust particles, the smallest of the boulders, floated out across the whole breadth of the valley and formed a ceiling that lasted until after sunrise; and the air was loaded with the odor of crushed Douglas spruces, from a grove that had been mowed down and mashed like weeds.

Sauntering about to see what other changes had been made, I found the Indians in the middle of the valley, terribly frightened, of course, fearing the angry spirits of the rocks were trying to kill them. The few whites winter-

(continued on p.71)

While subterranean shiftings sometimes change mountains (opposite), external forces such as glaciers also altered rocks, such as this polished slab (right).

ing in the valley were assembled in front of the old Hutchings Hotel, comparing notes and meditating flight to steadier ground, seemingly as sorely frightened as the Indians. It is always interesting to see people in dead earnest, from whatever cause, and earthquakes make everybody earnest. Shortly after sunrise, a low blunt muffled rumbling, like distant thunder, was followed by another series of shocks, which, though not nearly so severe as the first, made the cliffs and domes tremble like jelly, and the big pines and oaks thrill and swish and wave their branches with startling effect. Then the groups of talkers were suddenly hushed, and the solemnity of their faces was sublime. One in particular of these winter neighbors, a rather thoughtful, speculative man, with whom I had often conversed, was a firm believer in the cataclysmic origin of the valley; and I now jokingly remarked that his wild tumble-down-and-engulfment hypothesis might soon be proved, since these underground rumblings and shakings might be the forerunners of another Yosemite-making cataclysm, which would perhaps double the depth of the valley by swallowing the floor, leaving the ends of the wagon roads and trails three or four thousand feet in the air. Just then came the second series of shocks, and it was fine to see how awfully silent and solemn he became. His belief in the existence of a mysterious abyss, into which the suspended floor of the valley and all the domes and battlements of the walls might at any moment go roaring down, mightily troubled him. To cheer and tease him into another view of the case, I said: "Come, cheer up; smile a little and clap your hands, now that kind Mother Earth is trotting us on her knee to amuse us and make us good." But the well-meant joke seemed irreverent and utterly failed, as if only prayerful terror could rightly belong to the wild beauty-making business. Even after all the heavier shocks were over, I could do nothing to reassure him. On the contrary, he handed me the keys of his little store, and, with a companion of like mind, fled to the lowlands. In about a month he returned; but a sharp shock occurred that very day, which sent him flying again.

The rocks trembled more or less every day for over two months, and I kept a bucket of water on my table to learn what I could of the movements. The blunt thunder-tones in the depths of the mountains were usually followed by sudden jarring, horizontal thrusts from the northward, often succeeded by twisting, upjolting movements. Judging by its effects, this Yosemite, or Inyo earthquake, as it is sometimes called, was gentle as compared with the one that gave rise to the grand talus system of the range and did so much for the cañon scenery. Nature, usually so deliberate in her operations, then created, as we have seen, a new set of features, simply by giving the mountains a shake — changing not only the high peaks and cliffs, but the streams. As soon as these rock avalanches fell every stream began to sing new songs; for in many places thousands of boulders were hurled into their channels, roughening and half damming them, compelling the waters to surge and roar in rapids where before they were gliding smoothly. Some of the streams were completely dammed, driftwood, leaves, etc., filling the interstices between the boulders, thus giving rise to lakes and level reaches; and these, again, after being gradually filled in, to smooth meadows, through which the streams now silently meander; while at the same time some of the taluses took the places of old meadows and groves. Thus rough places were made smooth, and smooth places rough. But on the whole, by what at first sight seemed pure confusion and ruin, the landscapes were enriched; for gradually every talus, however big the boulders composing it, was covered with groves and gardens, and made a finely proportioned and ornamental base for the sheer cliffs. In this beauty work, every boulder is prepared and measured and put in its place more thoughtfully than are the stones of temples. If for a moment you are inclined to regard these taluses as mere draggled, chaotic dumps, climb to the top of one of them, tie your mountain shoes firmly over the instep, and with braced nerves run down without any haggling, puttering hesitation, boldly jumping from boulder to boulder with even speed. You will then find your feet playing a tune, and quickly discover the music and poetry of rock piles — a fine

Opposite: *Yellowstone: an uproar like avalanches and thunder.* Left: *"Storm-beaten sky gardens."*

lesson; and all nature's wildness tells the same story. Storms of every sort, torrents, earthquakes, cataclysms, "convulsions of nature," etc., however mysterious and lawless at first sight they may seem, are only harmonious notes in the song of creation, varied expressions of God's love.

Our National Parks

How boundless the day seems as we revel in these storm-beaten sky gardens amid so vast a congregation of onlooking mountains! Strange and admirable it is that the more savage and chilly and storm-chafed the mountains, the finer the glow on their faces and the finer the plants they bear. The myriads of flowers tinging the mountain-top do not seem to have grown out of the dry, rough gravel of disintegration, but rather they appear as visitors, a cloud of witnesses to Nature's love in what we in our timid ignorance and unbelief call howling desert. The surface of the ground, so dull and forbidding at first sight, besides being rich in plants, shines and sparkles with crystals: mica, hornblende, feldspar, quartz, tourmaline. The radiance in some places is so great as to be fairly dazzling, keen lance rays of every color flashing, sparkling in glorious abundance, joining the plants in their fine, brave beauty-work — every crystal, every flower a window opening into heaven, a mirror reflecting the Creator.

My First Summer in the Sierra

While tourists wait around a large geyser, . . . there is a chatter of small talk in anything but a solemn mood; and during the intervals between the preliminary splashes and upheavals some adventurer occasionally looks down the throat of the crater, admiring the silex formations and wondering whether Hades is as beautiful. But when, with awful uproar as if avalanches were falling and storms thundering in the depths, the tremendous outburst begins, all run away to a safe distance, and look on, awe-stricken and silent, in devout, worshipping wonder.

Our National Parks

How interesting to trace the history of a single raindrop! It is not long, geologically speaking, as we have seen, since the first raindrops fell on the newborn leafless Sierra landscapes. How different the lot of these falling now! Happy the showers that fall on so fair a wilderness — scarce a single drop can fail to find a beautiful spot — on the tops of the peaks, on the shining glacier pavements, on the great smooth domes, on forests and gardens and brushy moraines, plashing, glinting, pattering, laving. Some go to the high snowy fountains to swell their well-saved stores; some into the lakes, washing the mountain windows, patting their smooth glassy levels, making dimples and bubbles and spray; some into the waterfalls and cascades, as if eager to join in their dance and song and beat their foam yet finer; good luck and good work for the happy mountain raindrops, each one of them a high waterfall in itself, descending from the cliffs and hollows of the clouds to the cliffs and hollows of the rocks, out of the sky-thunder into the thunder of the falling rivers. Some, falling on meadows and bogs, creep silently out of sight to the grass roots, hiding softly as in a nest, slipping, oozing hither, thither, seeking and finding their appointed work. Some, descending through the spires of the woods, sift spray through the shining needles, whispering peace and good cheer to each one of them. Some drops with happy aim glint on the sides of crystals — quartz, hornblende, garnet, zircon, tourmaline, feldspar — patter on grains of gold and heavy way-worn nuggets; some, with blunt plap-plap and low bass drumming, fall on the broad leaves of veratrum, saxifrage, cypripedium. Some happy drops fall straight into the cups of flowers, kissing the lips of lilies. How far they have to go, how many cups to fill, great and small, cells too small to be seen, cups holding half a drop as well as lake basins between the hills, each replenished with equal care, every drop in all the blessed throng a silvery newborn star with lake and river, garden and grove, valley and mountain, all that the landscape holds reflected in its crystal depths, God's messenger, angel of love sent on its way with majesty and pomp and display of power that make man's greatest shows ridiculous.

Now the storm is over, the sky is clear, the last

rolling thunder-wave is spent on the peaks, and where are the raindrops now — what has become of all the shining throng? In winged vapor rising some are already hastening back to the sky, some have gone into the plants, creeping through invisible doors into the round rooms of cells, some are locked in crystals of ice, some in rock crystals, some in porous moraines to keep their small springs flowing, some have gone journeying on in the rivers to join the larger raindrop of the ocean. From form to form, beauty to beauty, ever changing, never resting, all are speeding on with love's enthusiasm, singing with the stars the eternal song of creation.

My First Summer in the Sierra

June 12 — A slight sprinkle of rain — large drops far apart, falling with hearty pat and plash on leaves and stones and into the mouths of flowers. Cumuli rising to the eastward. How beautiful their pearly bosses! How well they harmonize with the upswelling rocks beneath them. Mountains of the sky, solid-looking, finely sculptured, their richly varied topography wonderfully defined. Never before have I seen clouds so substantial looking in form and texture. Nearly every day toward noon they rise with visible swelling motion as if new worlds were being created. And how fondly they brood and hover over the gardens and forests with their cooling shadows and showers, keeping every petal and leaf in glad health and heart.

One may fancy the clouds themselves are plants, springing up in the sky-fields at the call of the sun, growing in beauty until they reach

(continued on p. 78)

Opposite: *"How deeply with beauty is beauty overlaid!"* such as bark covered with deer lichen. Below: *Two of America's most famous natural treasures: two huge granite slabs, El Capitan and Half Dome. Overleaf: Evening reflections, Jackson Lake, Grand Teton National Park: "What can poor mortals say about clouds?"*
David Muench

their prime, scattering rain and hail like berries and seeds, then wilting and dying.

My First Summer in the Sierra

Raindrops blossom brilliantly in the rainbow, and change to flowers in the sod, but snow comes in full flower direct from the dark frozen sky.

The Mountains of California

July 20 — Fine calm morning; air tense and clear; not the slightest breeze astir; everything shining, the rocks with wet crystals, the plants with dew, each receiving its portion of irised dewdrops and sunshine like living creatures getting their breakfast, their dew manna coming down from the starry sky like swarms of smaller stars. How wondrous fine are the particles in showers of dew, thousands required for a single drop, growing in the dark as silently as the grass! What pains are taken to keep this wilderness in health — showers of snow, showers of rain, showers of dew, floods of light, floods of invisible vapor, clouds, winds, all sorts of weather, interaction of plant on plant, animal on animal, etc., beyond thought! How fine Nature's methods! How deeply with beauty is beauty overlaid! the ground covered with crystals, the crystals with mosses and lichens and low-spreading grasses and flowers, these with larger plants leaf over leaf with ever-changing color and form, the broad palms of the firs outspread over these, the azure dome over all like a bell-flower, and star above star.

Yonder stands the South Dome, its crown high above our camp, though its base is four thousand feet below us; a most noble rock, it seems full of thought, clothed with living light, no sense of dead stone about it, all spiritualized, neither heavy looking nor light, steadfast in serene strength like a god.

My First Summer in the Sierra

July 23 — Another midday cloudland, displaying power and beauty that one never wearies in beholding, but hopelessly unsketchable and untellable. What can poor mortals say about clouds? While a description of their huge glowing domes and ridges, shadowy gulfs and cañons,

and feather-edged ravines is being tried, they vanish, leaving no visible ruins. Nevertheless, these fleeting sky mountains are as substantial and significant as the more lasting upheavals of granite beneath them. Both alike are built up and die, and in God's calendar difference of duration is nothing. We can only dream about them in wondering, worshipping admiration, happier than we dare tell even to friends who see farthest in sympathy, glad to know that not a crystal or vapor particle of them, hard or soft, is lost; that they sink and vanish only to rise again and again in higher and higher beauty. As to our own work, duty, influence, etc., concerning which so much fussy pother is made, it will not fail of its due effect, though, like a lichen on a stone, we keep silent.

My First Summer in the Sierra

In June small flecks of the dead, decaying sod begin to appear, gradually widening and uniting with one another, covered with creeping rags of water during the day, and ice by night, looking as hopeless and unvital as crushed rocks just emerging from the darkness of the glacial period. Walk the meadow now! Scarce the memory of a flower will you find. The ground seems twice dead. Nevertheless, the annual resurrection is drawing near. The life-giving sun pours his floods, the last snow-wreath melts, myriads of growing points push eagerly through the streaming mold, the birds come back, new wings fill the air, and fervid summer life comes surging on, seemingly yet more glorious than before.

The Mountains of California

August 27 — Contemplating the lace-like fabric of streams outspread over the mountains, we are reminded that everything is flowing — going somewhere, animals and so-called lifeless rocks as well as water. Thus the snow flows fast or slow in grand beauty-making glaciers and avalanches; the air in majestic floods carrying minerals, plant leaves, seeds, spores, with streams of music and fragrance; water streams carrying rocks both in solution and in the form of mud particles, sand, pebbles, and boulders. Rocks flow from volcanoes like water from springs, and

(continued on p. 81)

Frost formed on sides of Yosemite Falls.

animals flock together and flow in currents modified by stepping, leaping, gliding, flying, swimming, etc. While the stars go streaming through space pulsed on and on forever like blood globules in Nature's warm heart.

August 28 — The dawn a glorious song of color. Sky absolutely cloudless. A fine crop of hoarfrost. Warm after ten o'clock. The gentians don't mind the first frost though their petals seem so delicate; they close every night as if going to sleep, and awake fresh as ever in the morning sun-glory. The grass is a shade browner since last week, but there are no nipped wilted plants of any sort as far as I have seen. Butterflies and the grand host of smaller flies are benumbed every night, but they hover and dance in the sunbeams over the meadows before noon with no apparent lack of playful, joyful life. Soon they must all fall like petals in an orchard, dry and wrinkled, not a wing of all the mighty host left to tingle the air. Nevertheless new myriads will arise in the spring, rejoicing, exulting, as if laughing cold death to scorn.

August 29 — Clouds about .05, slight frost. Bland serene Indian summer weather. Have been gazing all day at the mountains, watching the changing lights. More and more plainly are they clothed with light as a garment, white tinged with pale purple, palest during the midday hours, richest in the morning and evening. Everything seems consciously peaceful, thoughtful, faithfully waiting God's will.

August 30 — This day just like yesterday. A few clouds motionless and apparently with no work to do beyond looking beautiful. Frost enough for crystal building — glorious fields of ice-diamonds destined to last but a night. How lavish is Nature building, pulling down, creating, destroying, chasing every material particle from form to form, ever changing, ever beautiful.

Mr. Delaney arrived this morning. Felt not a trace of loneliness while he was gone. On the contrary, I never enjoyed grander company. The whole wilderness seems to be alive and familiar, full of humanity. The very stones seem talkative, sympathetic, brotherly. No wonder when we consider that we all have the same Father and Mother.

My First Summer in the Sierra

81

Every clear frosty morning loud sounds are
heard booming and reverberating from side to
side of the Valley at intervals of a few minutes,
beginning soon after sunrise and continuing an
hour or two like a thunder-storm. In my first
winter in the Valley I could not make out the
source of this noise. I thought of falling boulders,
rock-blasting, etc. Not till I saw what looked like
hoarfrost dropping from the side of the Fall was
the problem explained. The strange thunder is
made by the fall of section of ice formed of spray
that is frozen on the face of the cliff along the
sides of the Upper Yosemite Fall — a sort of
crystal plaster, a foot or two thick, cracked off by
the sunbeams, awakening all the Valley like
cock-crowing, announcing the finest weather,
shouting aloud Nature's infinite industry and
love of hard work in creating beauty.

The Yosemite

The action of flowing ice, whether in the form of
river-like glaciers or broad mantles, especially
the part it played in sculpturing the earth, is as
yet but little understood. Water rivers work
openly where people dwell, and so does the rain,
and the sea, thundering on all the shores of the
world; and the universal ocean of air, though
invisible, speaks aloud in a thousand voices, and
explains its modes of working and its power. But

glaciers, back in their white solitudes, work
apart from men, exerting their tremendous
energies in silence and darkness. Outspread,
spirit-like, they brood above the predestined
landscapes, work on unwearied through immeasurable ages, until, in the fullness of time,
the mountains and valleys are brought forth,
channels furrowed for rivers, basins made for
lakes and meadows, and arms of the sea, soils
spread for forests and fields; then they shrink
and vanish like summer clouds.

The Yosemite

This change from icy darkness and death to
life and beauty was slow, as we count time, and
is still going on, north and south, over all the
world wherever glaciers exist. . . .

The Mountains of California

I watched the gestures of the pines while the
storm was at its height, and it was easy to see
that they were not distressed. Several large
sugar pines stood near the thicket in which I was
sheltered, bowing solemnly and tossing their
long arms as if interpreting the very words of the
storm while accepting its wildest onsets with
passionate exhilaration. The lions were feeding.
Those who have observed sunflowers feasting on
sunshine during the golden days of Indian summer know that none of their gestures express

thankfulness. Their celestial food is too heartily given, too heartily taken to leave room for thanks. The pines were evidently accepting the benefactions of the storm in the same whole-souled manner; and when I looked down among the budding hazels, and still lower to the young violets and fern tufts on the rocks, I noticed the same divine methods of giving and taking, and the same exquisite adaptations of what seems an outbreak of violent and uncontrollable force to the purposes of beautiful and delicate life. Calms like sleep come upon landscapes, just as they do on people and trees, and storms awaken them in the same way. In the dry midsummer of the lower portion of the range the withered hills and valleys seem to lie as empty and ex-pressionless as dead shells on a shore. Even the highest mountains may be found occasionally dull and uncommunicative as if in some way they had lost countenance and shrunk to less than half their real stature. But when the light-nings crash and echo in the cañons, and the clouds come down wreathing and crowning their bald snowy heads, every feature beams with expression and they rise again in all their imposing majesty.

Storms are fine speakers, and tell all they know, but their voices of lightning, torrent, and rushing wind are much less numerous than the nameless still, small voices too low for human ears; and because we are poor listeners we fail to catch much that is fairly within reach. Our best rains are heard mostly on roofs, and winds in chimneys; and when by choice or compulsion we are pushed into the heart of a storm, the con-fusion made by cumbersome equipments and nervous haste and mean fear, prevent our hear-ing any other than the loudest expressions. Yet we may draw enjoyment from storm sounds that are beyond hearing, and storm movements we cannot see. The sublime whirl of planets around their suns is as silent as raindrops oozing in the dark among the roots of plants. In this great storm, as in every other, there were tones and gestures inexpressibly gentle manifested in the midst of what is called violence and fury, but easily recognized by all who look and listen for them. . . .

When I arrived at the village about sundown the good people bestirred themselves, pitying my bedraggled condition as if I were some benumbed castaway snatched from the sea, while I, in turn, warm with excitement and reeking like the ground, pitied them for being dry and defrauded of all the glory that Nature had spread round about them that day.

The Mountains of California

The mountain winds, like the dew and rain, sunshine and snow, are measured and bestowed with love on the forests to develop their strength and beauty. However restricted the scope of other forest influences, that of the winds is universal. The snow bends and trims the upper forests every winter, the lightning strikes a single tree here and there, while avalanches mow down thousands at a swoop as a gardener trims out a bed of flowers. But the winds go to every tree, fingering every leaf and branch and furrowed bole; not one is forgotten; the mountain pine towering with outstretched arms on the rugged buttresses of the icy peaks, the lowliest and most retiring tenant of the dells; they seek and find them all, caressing them tenderly, bending them in lusty exercise, stimulating their growth, plucking off a leaf or limb as required, or removing an entire tree or grove, now whispering and cooing through the branches like a sleepy child, now roaring like the ocean; the winds blessing the forests, the forests the winds, with ineffable beauty and harmony as the sure result.

After one has seen pines six feet in diameter bending like grasses before a mountain gale, and ever and anon some giant falling with a crash that shakes the hills, it seems astonishing that any, save the lowest thickset trees, could ever have found a period sufficiently stormless to establish themselves; or, once established, that they should not, sooner or later, have been blown down. But when the storm is over, and we behold the same forests tranquil again, towering fresh and unscathed in erect majesty, and consider what centuries of storms have fallen upon them since they were first planted — hail, to break the tender seedlings; lightning, to scorch and shatter; snow, winds, and avalanches, to crush and overwhelm — while the manifest result of all this wild storm-culture is the glorious perfection we behold; then faith in Nature's forestry is established, and we cease to deplore the violence of her most destructive gales, or of any other storm-implement whatsoever. . . .

Toward midday, after a long, tingling scramble through copses of hazel and ceanothus,

I gained the summit of the highest ridge in the neighborhood; and then it occurred to me that it would be a fine thing to climb one of the trees to obtain a wider outlook and get my ear close to the Æolian music of its topmost needles. But under the circumstances the choice of a tree was a serious matter. One whose instep was not very strong seemed in danger of being blown down, or of being struck by others in case they should fall; another was branchless to a considerable height above the ground, and at the same time too large to be grasped with arms and legs in climbing; while others were not favorably situated for clear views. After cautiously casting about, I made choice of the tallest of a group of Douglas spruces that were growing close together like a tuft of grass, no one of which seemed likely to fall unless all the rest fell with it. Though comparatively young, they were about one hundred feet high, and their lithe, brushy tops were rocking and swirling in wild ecstasy. Being accustomed to climb trees in making botanical studies, I experienced no difficulty in reaching the top of this one, and never before did I enjoy so noble an exhilaration of motion. The slender tops fairly flapped and swished in the passionate torrent, bending and swirling backward and forward, round and round, tracing indescribable combinations of vertical and horizontal curves, while I clung with muscles firm braced, like a bobolink on a reed.

In its widest sweeps my tree-top described an arc of from twenty to thirty degrees, but I felt sure of its elastic temper, having seen others of the same species still more severely tried — bent almost to the ground indeed, in heavy snows — without breaking a fiber. I was therefore safe, and free to take the wind into my pulses and enjoy the excited forest from my superb outlook. The view from here must be extremely beautiful in any weather. Now my eye roved over the piny hills and dales as over fields of waving grain, and felt the light running in ripples and broad swelling undulations across the valleys from ridge to ridge, as the shining foliage was stirred by corresponding waves of air. Oftentimes these waves of reflected light would break up suddenly into a kind of beaten

foam, and again, after chasing one another in regular order, they would seem to bend forward in concentric curves, and disappear on some hillside, like sea waves on a shelving shore. The quantity of light reflected from the bent needles was so great as to make whole groves appear as if covered with snow, while the black shadows beneath the trees greatly enhanced the effect of the silvery splendor.

Excepting only the shadows there was nothing somber in all this wild sea of pines. On the contrary, notwithstanding this was the winter season, the colors were remarkably beautiful. The shafts of the pine and libocedrus were brown and purple, and most of the foliage was well tinged with yellow; the laurel groves, with the pale undersides of their leaves turned upward, made masses of gray; and then there was many a dash of chocolate color from clumps of manzanita, and jet of vivid crimson from the bark of the madroños, while the ground on the hillsides, appearing here and there through openings between the groves, displayed masses of pale purple and brown.

The sounds of the storm corresponded gloriously with this wild exuberance of light and motion. The profound bass of the naked branches and boles booming like waterfalls; the quick, tense vibrations of the pine needles, now rising to a shrill, whistling hiss, now falling to a silky murmur; the rustling of laurel groves in the dells, and the keen, metallic click of leaf on leaf — all this was heard in easy analysis when the attention was calmly bent.

The varied gestures of the multitude were seen to fine advantage, so that one could recognize the different species at a distance of several miles by this means alone, as well as by their forms and colors, and the way they reflected the light. All seemed strong and comfortable, as if really enjoying the storm, while responding to its most enthusiastic greetings. We hear much nowadays concerning the universal struggle for existence, but no struggle in the common meaning of the word was manifest here; no recognition of danger by any tree; no deprecation; but rather an invincible gladness as remote from exultation as from fear.

I kept my lofty perch for hours, frequently closing my eyes to enjoy the music by itself, or to feast quietly on the delicous fragrance that was streaming past. The fragrance of the woods was less marked than that produced during warm rain, when so many balsamic buds and leaves are steeped like tea; but, from the chafing of resiny branches against each other, and the incessant attrition of myriads of needles, the gale was spiced to a very tonic degree. And besides the fragrance from these local sources there were traces of scents brought from afar. For this wind came first from the sea, rubbing against its fresh, briny waves, then distilled through the redwoods, threading rich, ferny gulches, and spreading itself in broad, undulating currents over many a flower-enameled ridge of the coast mountains, then across the golden plains, up the purple foothills, and into these piny woods with the varied incense gathered by the way. . . .

We all travel the milky way together, trees and men; but it never occurred to me until this storm-day, while swinging in the wind, that trees are travelers, in the ordinary sense. They make many journeys, not extensive ones, it is true; but our own little journeys, away and back again, are only little more than tree-wavings — many of them not so much.

When the storm began to abate, I dismounted and sauntered down through the calming woods. The storm-tones died away, and, turning toward the east, I beheld the countless hosts of the forests hushed and tranquil, towering above one another on the slopes of the hills like a devout audience. The setting sun filled them with amber light, and seemed to say, while they listened, "My peace I give unto you."

As I gazed on the impressive scene, all the so-called ruin of the storm was forgotten, and never before did these noble woods appear so fresh, so joyous, so immortal.

The Mountains of California

Here [in a cave] we lingered and reveled, rejoicing to find so much music in stony silence, so much splendor in darkness, so many mansions in the depths of the mountains, buildings ever in process of construction, yet ever finished, developing from perfection to perfection, profusion without overabundance; every particle visible or invisible in glorious motion, marching to the music of the spheres in a region regarded as the abode of eternal stillness and death.

The outer chambers of mountain caves are frequently selected as homes by wild beasts. In the Sierra, however, they seem to prefer homes and hiding-places in chaparral and beneath shelving precipices, as I have never seen their tracks in any of the caves. This is the more remarkable because notwithstanding the darkness and oozing water there is nothing uncomfortably cellar-like or sepulchral about them.

When we emerged into the bright landscapes of the sun everything looked brighter, and we felt our faith in Nature's beauty strengthened, and saw more clearly that beauty is universal and immortal, above, beneath, on land and sea, mountain and plain, in heat and cold, light and darkness.

The Mountains of California

Walking quietly about . . . the Grand Canyon, . . . we learn something of the way it was made; and all must admire the effects so great from means apparently so simple, rain striking light hammer-blows or heavier in streams, with many rest Sundays; soft air and light, gentle sappers and miners, toiling forever; the big river sawing the plateau asunder, carrying away the eroded and ground waste, and exposing the edges of the strata to the weather; rain torrents sawing cross-streets and alleys, exposing the strata in the same way in hundreds of sections, the softer, less resisting beds weathering and receding

faster, thus undermining the harder beds, which fall, not only in small weathered particles, but in heavy sheer-cleaving masses, assisted down from time to time by kindly earthquakes, rain torrents rushing the fallen material to the river, keeping the wall rocks constantly exposed. Thus the cañon grows wider and deeper. So also do the side-cañons and amphitheaters, while secondary gorges and cirques gradually isolate masses of the promontories, forming new buildings, all of which are being weathered and pulled and shaken down while being built, showing destruction and creation as one. We see the proudest temples and palaces in stateliest attitudes, wearing their sheets of detritus as royal robes, shedding off showers of red and yellow stones like trees in autumn shedding their leaves, going to dust like beautiful days to night, proclaiming as with the tongues of angels the natural beauty of death.

Steep Trails

. . . And so this memorable month ends, a stream of beauty unmeasured, no more to be sectioned off by almanac arithmetic than sun-radiance or the currents of seas and rivers — a peaceful, joyful stream of beauty. Every morning, arising from the death of sleep, the happy plants and all our fellow animal creatures great and small, and even the rocks, seemed to be shouting, "Awake, awake, rejoice, rejoice, come love us and join in our song. Come! Come!" Looking back through the stillness and romantic enchanting beauty and peace of the camp grove, this June seems the greatest of all the months of my life, the most truly, divinely free, boundless like eternity, immortal. Everything in it seems equally divine — one smooth, pure, wild glow of Heaven's love, never to be blotted or blurred by anything past or to come.

My First Summer in the Sierra

But wheresoever we may venture to go in all this good world, nature is ever found richer and more beautiful than she seems, . . . amply sufficient throughout the barest deserts for a clear manifestation of God's love.

Steep Trails

Measureless Mountain Days

The mountains as well as the forests became home for John Muir. If the mountains happened to be forested, as they usually were, he was quite literally in heaven.

Although botany was Muir's first love, mountain geology ran a close second. He was particularly interested in glaciology. Much of his early writing was devoted to defending his idea that the Yosemite Valley and the other striking features of the Sierras were created primarily by glaciers.

The foremost geologists of his time maintained that Yosemite had been formed when the bottom dropped out suddenly in that area of instability in the earth's crust. Young Muir, without even a B.S. degree, arrived in California less than a year after seeing his first mountain and declared that all the experts were wrong. And they were. Muir attributed more influence to the glaciers than they actually had, but he analyzed the geology of the Sierras more accurately than any of his contemporaries.

Muir did prodigious feats of mountaineering to carry out his geological studies. But, in truth, geology was merely an interesting excuse for Muir to climb. He loved it and was invigorated by it. And, just as prophets of the Bible communed with God on the mountain tops, so did Muir.

Opposite: *Muir was an authority on the mountains of Yosemite, such as El Capitan, a favorite of climbers.*

The clear and invigorating mornings of the Sierra were always an inspiration to Muir.

Oh, these vast, calm, measureless mountain days, inciting at once to work and rest! Days in whose light everything seems equally divine, opening a thousand windows to show us God! Nevermore, however weary, should one faint by the way who gains the blessing of one mountain day; whatever his fate, long life, short life, stormy or calm, he is rich forever.

My First Summer in the Sierra

Another inspiring morning, nothing better in any world can be conceived. No description of Heaven that I have ever heard or read of seems half so fine.

My First Summer in the Sierra

Another glorious Sierra day in which one seems to be dissolved and absorbed and sent pulsing onward we know not where. Life seems neither long nor short, and we take no more heed to save time or make haste than do the trees and stars. This is true freedom, a good practical sort of immortality.

My First Summer in the Sierra

Have greatly enjoyed all this huge day, sauntering and seeing, steeping in the mountain influences, sketching, noting, pressing flowers. . . .

Sauntered up the meadow about sundown, out of sight of camp and sheep and all human mark, into the deep peace of the solemn old woods, everything glowing with Heaven's unquenchable enthusiasm.

My First Summer in the Sierra

July 26 — Ramble to the summit of Mt. Hoffman, eleven thousand feet high, the highest point in life's journey my feet have yet touched. And what glorious landscapes are about me, new plants, new animals, new crystals, and multitudes of new mountains far higher than Hoffman, towering in glorious array along the axis of the range, serene, majestic, snow-laden, sun-drenched, vast domes and ridges shining below them, forests, lakes, and meadows in the hollows, the pure blue bell-flower sky brooding them all — a glory day of admission into a new

realm of wonders as if Nature had wooingly whispered, "Come higher." What questions I asked, and how little I know of all the vast show, and how eagerly, tremulously hopeful of some day knowing more, learning the meaning of these divine symbols crowded together on this wondrous page.

My First Summer in the Sierra

Climb the mountains and get their good tidings. Nature's peace will flow into you as sunshine flows into trees. The winds will blow their own freshness into you, and the storms their energy, while cares will drip off like autumn leaves.

Our National Parks

The sky was perfectly delicious, sweet enough for the breath of angels; every draught of it gave a separate and distinct piece of pleasure. I do not believe that Adam and Eve ever tasted better in their balmiest nook.

A Thousand-Mile Walk to the Gulf

Toward sunset, enjoyed a fine run to camp, down the long south slopes, across ridges and ravines, gardens and avalanche gaps, through the firs and chaparral, enjoying wild excitement and excess of strength, and so ends a day that will never end.

My First Summer in the Sierra

In descending the divide to the main Kings River we made a descent of near seven thousand feet...to the hot pineless foothills. We rose again and it was a most grateful resurrection.

Letter to Mrs. Ezra S. Carr
October 2, 1873

We are now in the mountains and they are in us, kindling enthusiasm, making every nerve quiver, filling every pore and cell of us. Our flesh-and-bone tabernacle seems transparent as glass to the beauty about us, as if truly an inseparable part of it, thrilling with the air and trees, streams and rocks, in the waves of the sun — a part of all nature, neither old nor young, sick nor well, but immortal. Just now I can hardly conceive of any bodily condition dependent on food or breath any more than the ground or the sky. How glorious a conversion, so complete and wholesome it is, scarce memory enough of old bondage days left as a standpoint to view it from! In this newness of life we seem to have been so always.

Through a meadow opening in the pine woods I see snowy peaks about the headwaters of the Merced above Yosemite. How near they seem and how clear their outlines on the blue air, or rather *in* the blue air; for they seem to be saturated with it. How consuming strong the invitation they extend! Shall I be allowed to go to them? Night and day I'll pray that I may, but it seems too good to be true. Some one worthy will go, able for Godful work, yet as far as I can I must drift about these love-monument mountains, glad to be a servant of servants in so holy a wilderness.

Found a lovely lily (*Calochortus albus*) in a shady adenostoma thicket near Coulterville, in company with *Adiantum Chilense*. It is white with a faint purplish tinge inside at the base of the petals, a most impressive plant, pure as a snow crystal, one of the plant saints that all must love and be made so much purer by it every time it is seen. It puts the roughest mountaineer on his good behavior. With this plant the whole world would seem rich though none other existed. It is not easy to keep on with the camp cloud [of dust] while such plant people are standing preaching by the wayside.

...We are now approaching the region of clouds and cool streams. Magnificent white cumuli appeared about noon above the Yosemite region — floating fountains refreshing the glorious wilderness — sky mountains in whose pearly hills and dales the streams take their rise — blessing with cooling shadows and rain. No rock landscape is more varied in sculpture, none more delicately modeled than these landscapes of the sky; domes and peaks rising, swelling, white as finest marble and firmly outlined, a most impressive manifestation of world building. Every rain-cloud, however fleeting, leaves its mark, not only on trees and flowers whose pulses are quickened, and on the replenished streams and lakes, but also on the rocks are its marks engraved whether we can see them or not.

... [T]he weather is calm tonight, and our camp is only a sheep camp. We are near the North Fork of the Merced. The night wind is telling the wonders of the upper mountains, their snow fountains and gardens, forests and groves; even their topography is in its tones. And the stars, the everlasting sky lilies, how bright they are now that we have climbed above the lowland dust! The horizon is bounded and adorned by a spiry wall of pines, every tree harmoniously related to every other; definite symbols, divine hieroglyphics written with sunbeams. Would I could understand them! The stream flowing past the camp through ferns and lilies and alders makes sweet music to the ear, but the pines marshaled around the edge of the sky make a yet sweeter music to the eye. Divine beauty all. Here I could stay tethered forever with just bread and water, nor would I be lonely; loved friends and neighbors, as love for everything increased, would seem all the nearer however many the miles and mountains between us.

My First Summer in the Sierra

Wrote to my mother and a few friends, mountain hints to each. They seem as near as if within voice-reach or touch. The deeper the solitude the less the sense of loneliness, and the nearer our friends.

My First Summer in the Sierra

Somber peaks, hacked and shattered, circled halfway around the horizon, wearing a savage aspect in the gloaming, and a waterfall chanted solemnly across the lake on its way down from the foot of a glacier. The fall and the lake and the glacier were almost equally bare; while the scraggy pines anchored in the rock-fissures were so dwarfed and shorn by storm-winds that you might walk over their tops. In tone and aspect the scene was one of the most desolate I ever beheld. But the darkest scriptures of the mountains are illumined with bright passages of love that never fail to make themselves felt when one is alone.

The Mountains of California

[E]very step and jump on these blessed mountains is full of fine lessons.

My First Summer in the Sierra

[L]eaving wheels and animals out of the question, the free mountaineer with a sack of bread on his shoulders and an axe to cut steps in ice and frozen snow can make his way across the range almost everywhere, and at any time of year when the weather is calm. To him nearly every notch between the peaks is a pass, though much patient step-cutting is at times required up and down steeply inclined glaciers, with cautious climbing over precipices that at first sight would seem hopelessly inaccessible.

In pursuing my studies, I have crossed from side to side of the range at intervals of a few miles all along the highest portion of the chain, with far less real danger than one would naturally count on. And what fine wildness was thus revealed — storms and avalanches, lakes and waterfalls, gardens and meadows, and inter-

(continued on p. 98)

Wildflowers tinge the meadows of the Alabama Hills, looking toward 14,494-foot Mt. Whitney.

96

Opposite: *Very knowledgeable of mountain geology, Muir correctly attributed much of the Sierra's appearance to glacial action, contrary to his contemporaries. Upper Tenaya Canyon, Yosemite.*

esting animals — only those will ever know who give the freest and most buoyant portion of their lives to climbing and seeing for themselves.

To the timid traveler, fresh from the sedimentary levels of the lowlands, these highways, however picturesque and grand, seem terribly forbidding — cold, dead, gloomy gashes in the bones of the mountains, and of all Nature's ways the ones to be most cautiously avoided. Yet they are full of the finest and most telling examples of Nature's love; and though hard to travel, none are safer. For they lead through regions that lie far above the ordinary haunts of the devil, and of the pestilence that walks in darkness. True, there are innumerable places where the careless step will be the last step; and a rock falling from the cliffs may crush without warning like lightning from the sky; but what then? Accidents in the mountains are less common than in the lowlands, and these mountain mansions are decent, delightful, even divine, places to die in, compared with the doleful chambers of civilization. Few places in this world are more dangerous than home. Fear not, therefore, to try the mountain passes. They will kill care, save you from deadly apathy, set you free, and call forth every faculty into vigorous, enthusiastic action. Even the sick should try these so-called dangerous passes, because for every unfortunate they kill, they cure a thousand.

The Mountains of California

[T]he poor insignificant wanderer enjoys the freedom and glory of God's wilderness. . . . Wherever we go in the mountains, or indeed in any of God's wild fields, we find more than we seek.

My First Summer in the Sierra

The minister will not preach a perfectly flat and sedimentary sermon after climbing a snowy peak. . . .

Steep Trails

Narrow slot-like gorges extend across the summit at right angles, which look like lanes, formed evidently by the erosion of less resisting beds. They are usually called "devil's slides," though they lie far above the region usually haunted by the devil; for though we read that he once climbed an exceeding high mountain, he cannot be much of a mountaineer, for his tracks are seldom seen above the timberline.

My First Summer in the Sierra

To an observer upon this adamantine old monument in the midst of such scenery, getting glimpses of the thoughts of God, the day seems endless, the sun stands still. Much faithless fuss is made over the passage in the Bible telling of the standing still of the sun for Joshua. Here you may learn that the miracle occurs for every devout mountaineer, for everybody doing anything worth doing, seeing anything worth seeing. One day is as a thousand years, a thousand years as one day, and while yet in the flesh you enjoy immortality.

Our National Parks

On the way back to our Tuolumne camp, I enjoyed the scenery if possible more than when it first came to view. Every feature already seems familiar as if I had lived here always. I never weary gazing at the wonderful Cathedral. It has more individual character than any other rock or mountain I ever saw, excepting perhaps the Yosemite South Dome. The forests, too, seem kindly, familiar, and the lakes and meadows and glad singing streams. I should like to dwell with them forever. Here with bread and water I should be content. Even if not allowed to roam and climb, tethered to a stake or tree in some meadow or grove, even then I should be content forever. Bathed in such beauty, watching the expressions ever varying on the faces of the mountains, watching the stars, which here have a glory that the lowlander never dreams of, watching the circling seasons, listening to the songs of the waters and winds and birds, would be endless pleasure. And what glorious cloudlands I should see, storms and calms — a new heaven and a new earth every day, aye and new inhabitants. And how many visitors I should have. I feel sure I should not have one dull moment. And why should this appear extravagant? It is only common sense, a sign of

*Lower Yosemite Fall dropping down in snowy foam
from a mountain world to the valley floor.*

health, genuine, natural, all-awake health. One
would be at an endless godful play, and what
speeches and music and acting and scenery and
lights! — sun, moon, stars, auroras. Creation
just beginning, the morning stars "still singing
together and all the sons of God shouting
for joy."

My First Summer in the Sierra

[T]he word of God was being read in these
majestic hieroglyphics blazoned along the sky.
The earnest, childlike wonderment with which
this glorious page of Nature's Bible was con-
templated was delightful to see.

Travels in Alaska

Nearly all my mountaineering has been done
on foot, carrying as little as possible, depending
on camp-fires for warmth, that so I might
be light and free to go wherever my studies
might lead.

Our National Parks

No mountaineer is truly free who is trammeled
with friend or servant, or who has the care of
more than two legs. Besides, it seems cruel to
make any animal share one's toil without being
capable of sharing its rewards. What cared
Brownie for botany beyond grasses, or for landscapes beyond glacier meadows?

"The New Sequoia Forests of California"
Harper's Monthly, November 1878

I saw no mountains in all this grand region
that appeared at all inaccessible to a mountaineer. Give me a summer and a bunch of matches
and a sack of meal and I will climb every
mountain in the region.

Letter to Mrs. Ezra S. Carr
October 17, 1873

Falling rocks, single or in avalanches, form the
greatest of all the perils that beset the mountaineer among the summit peaks.

San Francisco Daily Evening Bulletin
August 24, 1875

I rambled along the valley rim to the westward; most of it is rounded off on the very brink,
so that it is not easy to find places where one
may look clear down the face of the wall to the

Thompson Lake is one of the Sierras' highest.

bottom. When such places were found, and I had cautiously set my feet and drawn my body erect, I could not help fearing a little that the rock might split off and let me down, and what a down! — more than three thousand feet. Still my limbs did not tremble, nor did I feel the least uncertainty as to the reliance to be placed on them. My only fear was that a flake of the granite, which in some places showed joints more or less open and running parallel with the face of the cliff, might give way. After withdrawing from such places, excited with the view I had got, I would say to myself, "Now don't go out on the verge again." But in the face of Yosemite scenery cautious remonstrance is vain; under its spell one's body seems to go where it likes with a will over which we seem to have scarce any control.

After a mile or so of this memorable cliff work I approached Yosemite Creek, admiring its easy, graceful, confident gestures as it comes bravely forward in its narrow channel, singing the last of its mountain songs on its way to its fate — a few rods more over the shining granite, then down half a mile in snowy foam to another world, to be lost in the Merced, where climate, vegetation,

inhabitants, all are different. Emerging from its last gorge, it glides in wide lace-like rapids down a smooth incline into a pool where it seems to rest and compose its gray, agitated waters before taking the grand plunge, then slowly slipping over the lip of the pool basin, it descends another glossy slope with rapidly accelerated speed to the brink of the tremendous cliff, and with sublime, fateful confidence springs out free in the air.

I took off my shoes and stockings and worked my way cautiously down alongside the rushing flood, keeping my feet and hands pressed firmly on the polished rock. The booming, roaring water, rushing past close to my head, was very exciting. I had expected that the sloping apron would terminate with the perpendicular wall of the valley, and that from the foot of it, where it is less steeply inclined, I should be able to lean far enough out to see the forms and behavior of the fall all the way down to the bottom. But I found that there was yet another small brow over which I could not see, and which appeared to be too steep for mortal feet. Scanning it keenly, I discovered a narrow shelf about three inches wide on the very brink, just wide enough for a

"Beauty beyond thought everywhere, beneath, above, made and being made forever."

rest for one's heels. But there seemed to be no way of reaching it over so steep a brow. At length, after careful scrutiny of the surface, I found an irregular edge of a flake of the rock some distance back from the margin of the torrent. If I was to get down to the brink at all that rough edge, which might offer slight finger holds, was the only way. But the slope beside it looked dangerously smooth and steep, and the swift roaring flood beneath, overhead, and beside me way very nerve-trying. I therefore concluded not to venture farther, but did nevertheless. Tufts of artemisia were growing in clefts of the rock near by, and I filled my mouth with the bitter leaves, hoping they might help to prevent giddiness. Then, with a caution not known in ordinary circumstances, I crept down safely to the little ledge, got my heels well planted on it, then shuffled in a horizontal direction twenty or thirty feet until close to the outplunging current, which, by the time it had descended thus far, was already white. Here I obtained a perfectly free view down into the heart of the snowy, chanting throng of comet-like streamers, into which the body of the fall soon separates.

While perched on that narrow niche I was not distinctly conscious of danger. The tremendous grandeur of the fall in form and sound and motion, acting at close range, smothered the sense of fear, and in such places one's body takes keen care for safety on its own account. How long I remained down there, or how I returned, I can hardly tell. Anyhow I had a glorious time, and got back to camp about dark, enjoying triumphant exhilaration soon followed by dull weariness. Hereafter I'll try to keep from such extravagant, nerve-straining places. Yet such a day is well worth venturing for. My first view of the High Sierra, first view looking down into Yosemite, the death song of Yosemite Creek, and its flight over the vast cliff, each one of these is of itself enough for a great life-long landscape fortune — a most memorable day of days — enjoyment enough to kill if that were possible.

My First Summer in the Sierra

Few Yosemite visitors ever see snow avalanches and fewer still know the exhilaration of riding on them. In all my mountaineering I have enjoyed only one avalanche ride, and the start was so sudden and the end came so soon I had but little time to think of the danger that attends this sort of travel, though at such times one thinks fast. One fine Yosemite morning after a heavy snowfall, being eager to see as many avalanches as possible and wide views of the forest and summit peaks in their new white robes before the sunshine had time to change them, I set out early to climb by a side cañon to the top of a commanding ridge a little over three thousand feet above the Valley. On account of the looseness of the snow that blocked the canyon I knew the climb would require a long time, some three or four hours as I estimated; but it proved far more difficult than I had anticipated. Most of the way I sank waist deep, almost out of sight in some places. After spending the whole day to within half an hour or so of sundown, I was still several hundred feet below the summit. Then my hopes were reduced to getting up in time to see the sunset. But I was not to get summit views of any sort that day, for deep trampling near the cañon head, where the snow was strained, started an avalanche, and I was swished down to the foot of the cañon as if by enchantment. The wallowing ascent had taken nearly all day, the descent only about a minute. When the avalanche started I threw myself on my back and spread my arms to try to keep from sinking. Fortunately, though the grade of the cañon is very steep, it is not interrupted by precipices large enough to cause outbounding or free plunging. On no part of the rush was I buried. I was only moderately imbedded on the surface or at times a little below it, and covered with a veil of back-streaming dust particles; and as the whole mass beneath me joined in the flight there was no friction, though I was tossed here and there and lurched from side to side. When the avalanche . . . came to rest I found myself on top of the crumpled pile without a bruise or scar. This was a fine experience. Hawthorne says somewhere that steam has spiritualized travel; though unspiritual smells, smoke, etc., still attend steam travel. This flight in what might be called a milky way of snow-stars was the most spiritual and exhilarating of all the modes of motion I have

ever experienced. Elijah's flight in a chariot of fire could hardly have been more gloriously exciting.

The Yosemite

God cares for us as long as we are trustful and brave. . . .

Travels in Alaska

No lowlander can appreciate the mountain appetite, and the facility with which heavy food called "grub" is disposed of. Eating, walking, resting, seem alike delightful, and one feels inclined to shout lustily on rising in the morning like a crowing cock. Sleep and digestion as clear as the air.

My First Summer in the Sierra

I was terribly hungry ere I got out of this wild cañon — had less than sufficient for one meal in the last four days, and this, coupled with very hard nerve-trying cliff work was sufficiently exhausting for any mountaineer. Yet strange to say, I did not suffer much. Crystal water, and air, and honey sucked from the scarlet flowers of zauschneria, about one-tenth as much as would suffice a hummingbird, was my last breakfast — a very temperate meal, was it not? — wholly ungross and very nearly spiritual. The last effort before reaching food was a climb up out of the main cañon of five thousand feet. Still I made it in fair time — only a little faint, no giddiness, want of spirit, or incapacity to observe and enjoy, or any nonsense of this kind. How I should have liked to have then tumbled into your care for a day or two!

To Mrs. John Bidwell in a letter to her husband
December 3, 1877

The Mountains of California

Besides herding the sheep, Billy is the butcher, while I have agreed to wash the few iron and tin utensils and make the bread. Then, these small duties done, by the time the sun is fairly above the mountain-tops I am beyond the flock, free to rove and revel in the wilderness all the big immortal days.

Sketching on the North Dome. It commands views of nearly all the valley besides a few of the high mountains. I would fain draw everything in sight — rock, tree, and leaf. But little can I do beyond mere outlines — marks with meanings like words, readable only to myself — yet I sharpen my pencils and work on as if others might possibly be benefited. Whether these picture-sheets are to vanish like fallen leaves or go to friends like letters, matters not much; for little can they tell to those who have not themselves seen similar wildness, and like a language have learned it. No pain here, no dull empty hours, no fear of the past, no fear of the future. These blessed mountains are so compactly filled with God's beauty, no petty personal hope or experience has room to be. Drinking this champagne water is pure pleasure, so is breathing the living air, and every movement of limbs is pleasure, while the whole body seems to feel beauty when exposed to it as it feels the campfire or sunshine, entering not by the eyes alone, but equally through all one's flesh like radiant heat, making a passionate ecstatic pleasure-glow not explainable. One's body then seems homogeneous throughout, sound as a crystal.

Perched like a fly on this Yosemite dome, I gaze and sketch and bask, oftentimes settling down into dumb admiration without definite hope of ever learning much, yet with longing, unresting effort that lies at the door of hope, humbly prostrate before the vast display of God's power, and eager to offer self-denial and renunciation with eternal toil to learn any lesson in the divine manuscript.

It is easier to feel than to realize, or in any way explain Yosemite grandeur. The magnitudes of the rocks and trees and streams are so delicately harmonized they are mostly hidden. Sheer precipices three thousand feet high are fringed with tall trees growing close like grass on the brow of a lowland hill, and extending along the feet of these precipices a ribbon of meadow a mile wide and seven or eight long, that seems like a strip a farmer might mow in less than a day. Waterfalls, five hundred to one or two thousand feet high, are so subordinated to the mighty cliffs over which they pour that they seem like wisps of smoke, gentle as floating clouds, though their voices fill the valley and make the rocks tremble. The mountains, too, along the eastern sky, and the domes in front of them, and the succession of smooth rounded waves between, swelling higher, higher, with dark woods in their hollows, serene in massive exuberant bulk and beauty, tend yet more to hide the grandeur of the Yosemite temple and make it appear as a subdued subordinate feature of the vast harmonious landscape. Thus every attempt to appreciate any one feature is beaten down by

Emerald Bay, Lake Tahoe: "The mountains are calling me and I must go. . . ."

the overwhelming influence of all the others. And, as if this were not enough, lo! in the sky arises another mountain range with topography as rugged and substantial-looking as the one beneath it — snowy peaks and domes and shadowy Yosemite valleys — another version of the snowy Sierra, a new creation heralded by a thunder-storm. How fiercely, devoutly wild is Nature in the midst of her beauty-loving tenderness! — painting lilies, watering them, caressing them with gentle hand, going from flower to flower like a gardener while building rock mountains and cloud mountains full of lightning and rain. Gladly we run for shelter beneath an overhanging cliff and examine the reassuring ferns and mosses, gentle love tokens growing in cracks and chinks. Daisies, too, and ivesias, confiding wild children of light, too small to fear. To these one's heart goes home, and the voices of the storm become gentle. Now the sun breaks forth and fragrant steam arises. The birds are out singing on the edges of the groves. The west

Above: *Mountain sheep: "Like the true mountaineers they are, they never seem to hurry."* Right: *Sunset in Rock Creek Canyon, the central Sierras: "Steeping in the mountain influences . . . ."*

is flaming in gold and purple, ready for the ceremony of the sunset, and back I go to camp with my notes and pictures, the best of them printed in my mind as dreams. A fruitful day, without measured beginning or ending. A terrestrial eternity. A gift of good God.

My First Summer in the Sierra

I have just returned from the longest and hardest trip I have ever made in the mountains, having been gone over five weeks. I am weary, but resting fast; sleepy, but sleeping deep and fast; hungry, but eating much. For two weeks I explored the glaciers of the summits east of here, sleeping among the snowy mountains without blankets and with but little to eat on account of its being so inaccessible. After my icy experiences it seems strange to be down here in so warm and flowery a climate.

I will soon be off again, determined to use all the seaon in prosecuting my researches — will go next to Kings River a hundred miles south,

then to Lake Tahoe and adjacent mountains, and in winter work in Oakland with my pen.

The Scotch are slow, but some day I will have the results of my mountain studies in a form in which you all will be able to read and judge of them. . . . The mountains are calling and I must go. . . .

Letter to his sister, Sarah Muir Galloway, from Yosemite Valley, September 3, 1873

The sculpture of the landscape is as striking in its main lines as in its lavish richness of detail; a grand congregation of massive heights with the river shining between, each carved into smooth graceful folds without leaving a single rocky angle exposed, as if the delicate fluting and ridging fashioned out of metamorphic slates had been carefully sandpapered. The whole landscape showed design, like man's noblest sculptures. How wonderful the power of its beauty! Gazing awe-stricken, I might have left everything for it. Glad, endless work would then be mine

zigzag. They were in full sight at first, only forty yards distant, and seemed to have been scattered; two or three were on my left on the opposite side of the cascades. Had they been tame sheep, they would have run off to destruction. This first lovely fellow studied the intentions of the flock, and met them by making leaps on glacial bosses that made me hold my breath. They first had to cross loose angular blocks of granite, which they did spendidly; then they leaped up the face of the mountain just where I thought they wouldn't, and perhaps couldn't go. I could have scaled the same precipice, but not where they did. I could have followed in most places only by being barefooted.

Like the true mountaineers they are, they never seem to hurry. They went up over the polished bosses in admirable order and with no noise, each showing a separate will, some lingering to look back at me, some hastening on to the front. Each individual crossed the river, unlike tame sheep. Tame sheep often jump at a rock face and fall back, but here was not one false step. These are clean and elegant, the others dirty and awkward. These are guarded by the Great Shepherd of us all, those by erring money-seekers. They passed in review before me; so also did deer — the sheep for the rocks and rough mountain work, the deer for the forest and green grassy meadows.

Looking at them I often cried out, "That was good!" . . . I exulted in the power and sufficiency of Nature, and felt like saying aloud to God as to a man, "Well done!"

John of the Mountains

tracing the forces that have brought forth its features, its rocks and plants and animals and glorious weather. Beauty beyond thought everywhere, beneath, above, made and being made forever. I gazed and gazed and longed and admired until the dusty sheep and packs were far out of sight, made hurried notes and a sketch, though there was no need of either, for the colors and lines and expressions of this divine landscape-countenance are so burned into my mind and heart they surely can never grow dim.

My First Summer in the Sierra

I saw a fine band of mountain sheep, light gray in color, white on the backs of hips, with black tails. All horned, they seemed strong and moved with great deliberation, led by the largest. They crossed the river between the steps of the cascade where the channel was blocked and bridged with big boulders. On level ground they were close together, but in ascending the steep mountain wall were far apart in single file,

The wild sheep ranks among the noblest of animal mountaineers. . . . [T]hey bring forth their young, in the most solitary and inaccessible crags, far above the nest of the eagle. I have frequently come upon the beds of the ewes and lambs at an elevation of from 12,000 to 13,000 feet above sea level. These beds consist simply of an oval-shaped hollow, pawed out among loose disintegrating rock chips and sand, upon some sunny spot commanding a good outlook, and partially sheltered from the winds that sweep passionately across those lofty crags almost without intermission. Such is the cradle

Pikas (above), which seldom weigh more than seven ounces, are members of the same family as rabbits. They are sometimes confused with woodchucks (opposite) and marmots, larger animals of the squirrel family. Pikas and marmots are both denizens of the Western and Alaskan mountains.

of the little mountaineer, aloft in the sky, rocked in storms, curtained in clouds, sleeping in thin, icy air; but wrapped in his hairy coat, nourished by a warm, strong mother, defended from the talons of the eagle and teeth of sly coyote, the bonnie lamb grows apace. He learns to nibble the purple daisy and leaves of the white spiraea; his horns begin to shoot, and ere summer is done, he is strong and agile, and goes forth with the flock, shepherded by the same Divine love that tends the more helpless human lamb in its warm cradle by the fireside.

Steep Trails

I caught sight, for the first time, of the curious pika, or little chief hare, that cuts large quantities of lupines and other plants and lays them out to dry in the sun for hay, which it stores in underground barns to last through the long, snowy winter. Coming upon the plants freshly cut and lying in handfuls here and there on the rocks has a startling effect of busy life on the lonely mountain-top. These little haymakers, endowed with brain stuff something like our own — God up here looking after them — what lessons they teach, how they widen our sympathy!

My First Summer in the Sierra

Deer are capital mountaineers, making their way into the heart of the roughest mountains; seeking not only pasturage, but a cool climate, and safe hidden places in which to bring forth their young.

Our National Parks

I like to watch the squirrels. There are two species here, the large California gray and the Douglas. The latter is the brightest of all the squirrels I have ever seen, a hot spark of life, making every tree tingle with his prickly toes, a condensed nugget of fresh mountain vigor and valor, as free from disease as a sunbeam. One cannot think of such an animal ever being weary or sick. He seems to think the mountains belong to him, and at first tried to drive away the whole flock of sheep as well as the shepherd and dogs.

My First Summer in the Sierra

The woodchuck (*Arctomys monax*) dwells on high bleak ridges and boulder piles; and a very different sort of mountaineer is he — bulky, fat, aldermanic, and fairly bloated at times by hearty indulgence in the lush pastures of his airy home. And yet he is by no means a dull animal. In the midst of what we regard as storm-beaten desolation, high in the frosty air, beside the

glaciers he pipes and whistles right cheerily and lives to a good old age. If you are as early a riser as he is, you may oftentimes see him come blinking out of his burrow to meet the first beams of the morning and take a sunbath on some favorite flat-topped boulder. Afterward, well warmed, he goes to breakfast in one of his garden hollows, eats heartily like a cow in clover until comfortably swollen, then goes avisiting, and plays and loves and fights. . . .

Our National Parks

In the spring, after all the avalanches are down and the snow is melting fast, it is glorious to hear the streams sing out on the mountains.

Our National Parks

There is nothing more eloquent in Nature than a mountain stream, and this is the first I ever saw. Its banks are luxuriantly peopled with rare and lovely flowers and over arching trees, making one of Nature's coolest and most hospitable places.

A Thousand-Mile Walk to the Gulf

The basin of this famous Yosemite stream is extremely rocky — seems fairly to be paved with domes like a street with big cobblestones. I wonder if I shall ever be allowed to explore it. It draws me strongly, I would make any sacrifice to try to read its lessons. I thank God for this glimpse of it. The charms of these mountains are beyond all common reason, unexplainable and mysterious as life itself.

My First Summer in the Sierra

From the margin of these glorious forests the first general view of the Valley used to be gained — a revelation in landscape affairs that enriches one's life forever. Entering the Valley, gazing overwhelmed with the multitude of grand objects about us, perhaps the first to fix our attention will be the Bridal Veil, a beautiful waterfall on our right. Its brow, where it first leaps free from the cliff, is about nine hundred feet above us; and as it sways and sings in the wind, clad in gauzy, sun-sifted spray, half falling, half floating, it seems infinitely gentle and fine; but the hymns it sings tell the solemn, fateful power hidden beneath its soft clothing.

The Yosemite

From this long, flowery, forested well-watered park the walls rise abruptly in plain precipices or richly sculptured masses partly separated by side cañons, displaying wonderful wealth and variety of architectural forms, which are as wonderful in beauty of color and fineness of finish as in colossal height and mass. The so-called war of the elements has done them no harm. There is no unsightly defacement as yet; deep in the sky, inviting the onset of storms through unnumbered centuries, they still stand firm and seemingly as fresh and unworn as newborn flowers. . . . [I]t is an Eden of plant-beauty from end to end.

"A Rival of the Yosemite"
Century Magazine, November 1891

It is hard without long and loving study to realize the magnitude of the work done on these mountains during the last glacial period by glaciers, which are only streams of closely compacted snow-crystals. Careful study of the phenomena presented goes to show that the pre-glacial condition of the range was comparatively simple: one vast wave of stone in which a thousand mountains, domes, cañons, ridges, etc., lay concealed. And in the development of these Nature chose for a tool not the earthquake or lightning to rend and split asunder, not the stormy torrent or eroding rain, but the tender snow-flowers noiselessly falling through unnumbered centuries, the offspring of the sun and sea. Laboring harmoniously in united strength they crushed and ground and wore away the rocks in their march, making vast beds of soil, and at the same time developed and fashioned the landscapes into the delightful variety of hill and dale and lordly mountain that mortals call beauty. Perhaps more than a mile in average depth has the range been thus degraded during the last glacial period — a quantity of mechanical work almost inconceivably great. And our admiration must be excited again and again as we toil and study and learn that this vast job of rockwork, so

far-reaching in its influences, was done by agents so fragile and small as are these flowers of the mountain clouds. Strong only by force of numbers, they carried away entire mountains, particle by particle, block by block, and cast them into the sea; sculptured, fashioned, modeled all the range, and developed its predestined beauty. All these new Sierra landscapes were evidently predestined, for the physical structure of the rocks on which the features of the scenery depend was acquired while they lay at least a mile deep below the pre-glacial surface. And it was while these features were taking form in the depths of the range, the particles of the rocks marching to their appointed places in the dark with reference to the coming beauty, that the particles of icy vapor in the sky marching to the same music assembled to bring them to the light. Then, after their grand task was done, these bands of snow-flowers, these mighty glaciers, were melted and removed as if of no more importance than dew destined to last but an hour.

The Mountains of California

How fully are all the forms and languages of water, sands, trees, flowers, birds, rocks, subordinated to the primary structure of the mountains ere they were ice-sculptured! When all was planned and ready, snow-flowers were dusted over them, forming a film of ice over the mountain plate. And so all this development — the photography of God. . . .

John of the Mountains

A Very Strong-Minded Man

Although the differences between John Muir and his father were as wide and deep as the Grand Canyon, there were also similarities. Both were filled with religious zeal which generated strong opinions in them. And neither was shy about defending his opinions against anyone, especially against each other. Since they rarely agreed about anything, they usually were in conflict, for neither would back down. It probably was fortunate that half a continent separated them during most of John's adult years.

But leaving home did not end conflict for John Muir. From college to the end of his life, he had a reputation as a brilliant debater. He seemed to be able to argue without making his opponents angry. At least he was much in demand at all sorts of social events and meetings in California merely because it was expected that the conversation would be lively and interesting if John Muir were present. Once he was offered one hundred dollars just to attend a Sunday school convention and converse.

Although many persons sought Muir's company and regarded his words highly, it is difficult to believe that his strong opinions endeared him to everyone. There is no indication that he deliberately adopted the personality of Old Testament prophets, but he certainly performed a similar role in his own society.

Prophets are never universally popular. Muir was ready and willing to remind men individually or mankind in general of their sins, and especially of their subordinate role in relation to the Creator. He was witty, at times sarcastic. To some men at least he must have been very irritating.

But he did not condemn constantly. Most of his influence was of the kind that made people see good where they had not seen it before. Condemnation was reserved for those who refused to see the good and who arrogantly, selfishly set out to destroy it.

*Congressman William Kent (right) greatly admired Muir (left). Kent's dona-
tion to the government of coastal redwoods is now Muir National Monument.*

Muir's successes, and those of the Sierra Club which he founded,
indicated that America could respond to a prophetic call for justice
and righteousness. One of the first Americans to respond to Muir's
prophetic persuasion was a backwoods blacksmith that Muir met
while walking from Indiana to the Gulf of Mexico. The blacksmith
soon observed what all who came in contact with Muir quickly
learned — he was ''a very strong-minded man.''

Arriving at the last house, my knock at the door was answered by a bright, good-natured, good-looking little woman, who in reply to my request for a night's lodging and food, said, "Oh, I guess so. I think you can stay. Come in and I'll call my husband." "But I must first warn you," I said, "that I have nothing smaller to offer you than a five-dollar bill for my entertainment. I don't want you to think that I am trying to impose on your hospitality."

She then called her husband, a blacksmith, who was at work at his forge. He came out, hammer in hand, bare-breasted, sweaty, be-grimed, and covered with shaggy black hair. In reply to his wife's statement, that this young man wished to stop over night, he quickly replied, "That's all right; tell him to go into the house." He was turning to go back to his shop, when his wife added, "But he says he hasn't any change to pay. He has nothing smaller than a five-dollar bill." Hesitating only a moment, he turned on his heel and said, "Tell him to go into the house. A man that comes right out like that beforehand is welcome to eat my bread."

When he came in after his hard day's work and sat down to dinner, he solemnly asked a blessing

Yellow pond lilies: Muir often quoted Christ's admonition to his disciples: "Consider the lilies."

down here to these Southern States to get acquainted with as many of them as possible."

"You look like a strong-minded man," he replied, "and surely you are able to do something better than wander over the country and look at weeds and blossoms. These are hard times, and real work is required of every man that is able. Picking up blossoms doesn't seem to be a man's work at all in any kind of times."

To this I replied, "You are a believer in the Bible, are you not?" "Oh, yes." "Well, you know Solomon was a strong-minded man, and he is generally believed to have been the very wisest man the world ever saw, and yet he considered it was worthwhile to study plants; not only to go and pick them up as I am doing, but to study them; and you know we are told that he wrote a book about plants, not only of the great cedars of Lebanon, but of little bits of things growing in the cracks of the walls.

"Therefore, you see that Solomon differed very much more from you than from me in this matter. I'll warrant you he had many a long ramble in the mountains of Judea, and had he been a Yankee he would likely have visited every weed in the land. And again, do you not remember that Christ told his disciples to 'consider the lilies how they grow,' and compared their beauty with Solomon in all his glory? Now, whose advice am I to take, yours or Christ's? Christ says, 'Consider the lilies.' You say, 'Don't consider them. It isn't worthwhile for any strong-minded man.' "

This evidently satisfied him, and he acknowledged that he had never thought of blossoms in that way before. He repeated again and again that I must be a very strong-minded man, and admitted that no doubt I was fully justified in picking up blossoms.

A Thousand-Mile Walk to the Gulf

September 19 — Camped this evening at Smith's Mill, on the first broad mountain bench or plateau reached in ascending the range, where pines grow large enough for good lumber. Here wheat, apples, peaches and grapes grow, and we were treated to wine and apples. The wine I didn't like, but Mr. Delaney and the

on the frugal meal, consisting solely of corn bread and bacon. Then, looking across the table at me, he said, "Young man, what are you doing down here?" I replied that I was looking at plants. "Plants? What kind of plants?" I said, "Oh, all kinds; grass, weeds, flowers, trees, mosses, ferns — almost everything that grows is interesting to me."

"Well, young man," he queried, "you mean to say that you are not employed by the Government on some private business?" "No," I said, "I am not employed by any one except just myself. I love all kinds of plants, and I came

117

The coyote (above) and black bear (opposite) are two animals that have thus far managed to survive the long predation by man that Muir thought savage.

Indian driver and the shepherd seemed to think the stuff divine. Compared to sparkling Sierra water fresh from heavens, it seemed a dull, muddy, stupid drink.

My First Summer in the Sierra

Interest in hunting is almost universal, so deeply is it rooted as an inherited instinct ever ready to rise and make itself known. Fine scenery may not stir a fiber of mind or body, but how quick and how true is the excitement of the pursuit of game! Then up flames the slumbering volcano of ancient wildness, all that has been done by church and school is for the moment destroyed, and the decent gentleman or devout saint becomes a howling, bloodthirsty, demented savage. It is not long since we all were cave-men and followed game for food as truly as wildcat or wolf, and the long repression of civilization seems to make the rebound to the

savage love of blood all the more violent. This frenzy, fortunately, does not last long in its most exaggerated form, and after a season of wildness refined gentlemen from cities are not more cruel than hunters and trappers who kill for a living.

Steep Trails

October 22 — This morning I was easily prevailed upon by the captain and an ex-judge, who was rusticating here, to join in a deer hunt. Had a delightful ramble in the long grass and flowery barrens. Started one deer but did not draw a single shot. The captain, the judge, and myself stood at different stations where the deer was expected to pass, while a brother of the captain entered the woods to arouse the game from cover. The one deer that he started took a direction different from any which this particular old buck had ever been known to take in times past, and in so doing was cordially cursed as being the "d---dest deer that ever ran unshot." To me it appeared as "d----dest" work to slaughter God's cattle for sport. "They were made for us," say these self-approving preachers; "for our food, our recreation, or other uses not yet discovered." As truthfully we might say on behalf of a bear, when he deals successfully with an unfortunate hunter, "Men and other bipeds were made for bears, and thanks be to God for claws and teeth so long."

Let a Christian hunter go to the Lord's woods and kill his well-kept beasts, or wild Indians, and it is well; but let an enterprising specimen of these proper, predestined victims go to houses and fields and kill the most worthless person of the vertical godlike killers — oh! that is horribly unorthodox, and on the part of the Indians atrocious murder! Well, I have precious little sympathy for the selfish propriety of civilized man, and if a war of races should occur between the wild beasts and Lord Man, I would be tempted to sympathize with the bears.

A Thousand-Mile Walk to the Gulf

The care-laden commercial lives we lead close our eyes to the operations of God as a workman, though openly carried on that all who will look may see.

Travels in Alaska

One must labor for beauty as for bread. . . .

The Yosemite

Travel-worn pioneers, who have been tossed about like boulders in flood-time, are thronging hither [San Gabriel Valley] as to a kind of terrestrial heaven, resolved to rest. They build, and plant, and settle, and so come under natural influences. When a man plants a tree he plants himself. . . . These and the seeds he plants, are his prayers, and, by them brought into right relations with God, he works greater miracles every day than ever were written.

Steep Trails

The drifts and tunnels in the rocks may perhaps be regarded as the prayers of the prospector, offered for the wealth he so earnestly craves; but, like prayers of any kind not in harmony with nature, they are not answered.

Steep Trails

Sheep, like people, are ungovernable when hungry. Excepting my guarded lily gardens, almost every leaf that these hoofed locusts can reach within a radius of a mile or two from camp has been devoured. Even the bushes are stripped bare, and in spite of dogs and shepherds the sheep scatter to all points of the compass and vanish in dust. I fear some are lost, for one of the sixteen black ones is missing.

June 17 — Counted the wool bundles this morning as they bounced through the narrow corral gate. About three hundred are missing, and as the shepherd could not go to seek them, I had to go. I tied a crust of bread to my belt, and with Carlo set out for the upper slopes of the Pilot Peak Ridge, and had a good day, notwithstanding the care of seeking the silly runaways. I went out for wool, and did not come back shorn. A peculiar light circled around the horizon, white and thin like that often seen over the auroral corona, blending into the blue of the upper sky. The only clouds were a few faint flossy pencilings like combed silk. I pushed direct to the boundary of the usual range of the flock, and around it until I found the outgoing trail of the wanderers. It led far up the ridge into an open place surrounded by a hedge-like growth of ceanothus chaparral. Carlo knew what I was about, and eagerly followed the scent until we came up to them, huddled in a timid, silent bunch. They had evidently been here all night and all the forenoon, afraid to go out to feed. Having escaped restraint, they were, like some people we know of, afraid of their freedom, did not know what to do with it, and seemed glad to get back into the old familiar bondage.

My First Summer in the Sierra

On through the forest ever higher we go, a cloud of dust dimming the way, thousands of feet, trampling leaves and flowers, but in this mighty wilderness they seem but a feeble band, and a thousand gardens will escape their blighting touch. They cannot hurt the trees, though some of the seedlings suffer, and should the woolly locusts be greatly multiplied, as on account of dollar value they are likely to be, then the forests, too, may in time be destroyed. Only the sky will then be safe, though hid from view by dust and smoke, incense of a bad sacrifice. Poor, helpless, hungry sheep, in great part misbegotten, without good right to be, semi-manufactured, made less by God than man, born out of time and place, yet their voices are strangely human and call out one's pity.

My First Summer in the Sierra

"Sheep-men" call azalea "sheep-poison," and wonder what the Creator was thinking about when he made it — so desperately does sheep business blind and degrade, though supposed to have had a refining influence in the good old days we read of. The California sheep-owner is in

Sheep-men once called the azalea "sheep-poison."

a haste to get rich. . . . Then indeed the wool is drawn close down over the poor fellow's eyes, dimming or shutting out almost everything worth seeing.

My First Summer in the Sierra

. . . [T]o think that the sheep should be allowed in these lily meadows! after how many centuries of Nature's care planting and watering them, tucking the bulbs in snugly below winter frost, shading the tender shoots with clouds drawn above them like curtains, pouring refreshing rain, making them perfect in beauty, and keeping them safe by a thousand miracles; yet, strange to say, allowing the trampling of devastating sheep. One might reasonably look for a wall of fire to fence such gardens. So extravagant is Nature with her choicest treasures, spending plant beauty as she spends sunshine, pouring it forth into land and sea, garden and desert. And so the beauty of lilies falls on angels and men, bears and squirrels, wolves and sheep, birds and bees, but as far as I have seen, man alone, and the animals he tames, destroy these gardens.

My First Summer in the Sierra

Aside from mere money profit one would rather herd wolves than sheep.

My First Summer in the Sierra

The drivers and dogs had a lively, laborious time getting the sheep across the creek, the second large stream thus far that they have been compelled to cross without a bridge; the first being the North Fork of the Merced near Bower Cave. Men and dogs, shouting and barking, drove the timid, water-fearing creatures in a close crowd against the bank, but not one of the flock would launch away. While thus jammed, the Don and the shepherd rushed through the frightened crowd to stampede those in front, but this would only cause a break backward, and away they would scamper through the stream-bank trees and scatter over the rocky pavement. Then with the aid of the dogs the runaways would again be gathered and made to face the stream, and again the compacted mass would break away, amid wild shouting and barking that might well have disturbed the stream itself and marred the music of its falls, to which visitors no doubt from all quarters of the globe were listening. "Hold them there!" shouted the Don; "the front ranks will soon tire of the pressure, and be glad to take to the water, then all will jump in and cross in a hurry." But they did nothing of the kind; they only avoided the pressure by breaking back in scores and hundreds, leaving the beauty of the banks sadly trampled.

If only one could be got to cross over, all would make haste to follow; but that one could not be found. A lamb was caught, carried across, and tied to a bush on the opposite bank, where it cried piteously for its mother. But though greatly concerned, the mother only called it back. That play on maternal affection failed, and we began to fear that we should be forced to make a long roundabout drive and cross the widespread tributaries of the creek in succession. This would require several days, but it had its advantages, for I was eager to see the sources of so famous a stream. Don Quixote, however, determined that they must ford just here, and immediately began a sort of siege by cutting down slender pines on the bank and building a corral barely large enough to hold the flock when well pressed together. And as the stream would form one side of the corral he believed that they could easily be forced into the water.

In a few hours the inclosure was completed, and the silly animals were driven in and rammed hard against the brink of the ford. Then the Don, forcing a way through the compacted mass, pitched a few of the terrified unfortunates into the stream by main strength; but instead of crossing over, they swam about close to the bank, making desperate attempts to get back into the flock. Then a dozen or more were shoved off, and the Don, tall like a crane and a good natural wader, jumped in after them, seized a struggling wether, and dragged it to the opposite shore. But no sooner did he let it go than it jumped into the stream and swam back to its frightened companions in the corral, thus manifesting sheep-nature as unchangeable as gravitation. Pan with his pipes would have had no better luck, I fear. We were now pretty well baffled. The silly creatures would suffer any sort of death rather than cross that stream. Calling a council, the dripping Don declared that starvation was now the only likely scheme to try, and that we might as well camp here in comfort and let the besieged flock grow hungry and cool, and come to their senses, if they had any. In a few minutes after being thus let alone, an adventurer in the foremost rank plunged in and swam bravely to the farther shore. Then suddenly all rushed in pell-mell together, trampling one another under water, while we vainly tried to hold them back. The Don jumped into the thickest of the gasping, gurgling, drowning mass, and shoved them right and left as if each sheep was a piece of floating timber. The current also served to drift them apart; a long bent column was soon formed, and in a few minutes all were over and began baaing and feeding as if nothing out of the common had happened. . . .

As the day was far spent, we camped a little way back from the ford, and let the dripping flock scatter and feed until sundown. The wool is dry now, and calm, cud-chewing peace has fallen on all the comfortable band, leaving no trace of the watery battle. I have seen fish driven out of the water with less ado than was made in driving these animals into it. Sheep brain must surely be poor stuff. Compare today's exhibition with the performances of deer swimming quietly across broad and rapid rivers, and from island to island in seas and lakes; or with dogs, or even with the squirrels that, as the story goes, cross the Mississippi River on selected chips, with tails for sails comfortably trimmed to the breeze. A sheep can hardly be called an animal; an entire flock is required to make one foolish individual.

My First Summer in the Sierra

Our shepherd is a queer character and hard to place in this wilderness. His bed is a hollow made in red dry-rot punky dust beside a log which forms a portion of the south wall of the corral. Here he lies with his wonderful everlasting clothing on, wrapped in a red blanket, breathing not only the dust of the decayed wood but also that of the corral, as if determined to take ammoniacal snuff all night after chewing tobacco all day. Following the sheep he carries a heavy six-shooter swung from his belt on one side and his luncheon on the other. The ancient cloth in which the meat, fresh from the frying-pan, is tied serves as a filter through which the clear fat and gravy juices drip down on his right hip and leg in clustering stalactites. This oleaginous formation is soon broken up, however, and diffused and rubbed evenly into his scanty apparel, by sitting down, rolling over, crossing his legs while resting on logs, etc., making shirt and trousers water-tight and shiny. His trousers, in particular, have become so adhesive with the mixed fat and resin that pine needles,

Hetch Hetchy area: One can focus down on an agile mosaic-skinned lizard (above) or up to a waterfall mist on Wapama Rock (opposite).

thin flakes and fibres of bark, hair, mica scales and minute grains of quartz, hornblende, etc., feathers, seed wings, moth and butterfly wings, legs and antennae of innumerable insects, or even whole insects such as the small beetles, moths and mosquitoes, with flower petals, pollen dust and indeed bits of all plants, animals, and minerals of the region adhere to them and are safely imbedded, so that though far from being a naturalist, he collects fragmentary specimens of everything and becomes richer than he knows. His specimens are kept passably fresh, too, by the purity of the air and the resiny bituminous beds into which they are pressed. Man is a microcosm, at least our shepherd is, or rather his trousers. These precious overalls are never taken off, and nobody knows how old they are, though one may guess by their thickness and concentric structure. Instead of wearing thin they wear thick, and in their stratification have no small geological significance.

My First Summer in the Sierra

The artist. . .wandered day after day along the river and through the groves and gardens, studying the wonderful scenery; and, after making about forty sketches, declared with enthusiasm that although its walls were less sublime in height, in picturesque beauty and charm Hetch Hetchy surpassed even Yosemite.

That anyone would try to destroy such a place seems incredible; but sad experience shows that there are people good enough and bad enough for anything. The proponents of the dam scheme bring forward a lot of bad arguments to prove that the only righteous thing to do with the people's parks is to destroy them bit by bit as they are able. Their arguments are curiously like those of the devil, devised for the destruction of the first garden — so much of the very best Eden fruit going to waste. . . . Landscape gardens, places of recreation and worship, are never made beautiful by destroying and burying them.

Dam Hetch Hetchy! As well dam for water-tanks the people's cathedrals and churches, for no holier temple has ever been consecrated by the heart of man.

The Yosemite

The world, we are told, was made especially for man — a presumption not supported by all the facts. A numerous class of men are painfully astonished whenever they find anything, living or dead, in all God's universe, which they cannot eat or render in some way what they can call useful to themselves. They have precise dogmatic insight of the intentions of the Creator, and it is hardly possible to be guilty of irreverence in speaking of *their* God any more than of heathen idols. He is regarded as a civilized, law-abiding

gentleman in favor either of a republican form of government or of a limited monarchy; believes in the literature and language of England; is a warm supporter of the English constitution and Sunday schools and missionary societies; and is as purely a manufactured article as any puppet of a half-penny theater.

With such views of the Creator it is, of course, not surprising that erroneous views should be entertained of the creation. To such properly trimmed people, the sheep, for example, is an easy problem — food and clothing "for us," eating grass and daisies white by divine appointment for this predestined purpose, on perceiving the demand for wool that would be occasioned by the eating of the apple in the Garden of Eden.

In the same pleasant plan, whales are storehouses of oil for us, to help out the stars in lighting our dark ways until the discovery of the Pennsylvania oil wells. Among plants, hemp, to say nothing of the cereals, is a case of evident destination for ships' rigging, wrapping packages, and hanging the wicked. Cotton is another plain case of clothing. Iron was made for hammers and ploughs, and lead for bullets; all intended for us. And so of other small handfuls of insignificant things.

But if we should ask these profound expositors of God's intentions, How about those man-eating animals — lions, tigers, alligators — which smack their lips over raw man? Or about those myriads of noxious insects that destroy labor and drink his blood? Doubtless man was intended for food and drink for all these? Oh, no! Not at all! These are unresolvable difficulties connected with Eden's apple and the Devil. Why does water drown its lord? Why do so many minerals poison him? Why are so many plants and fishes deadly enemies? Why is the lord of

Above: *Diamondback rattlesnake, one of Muir's "poor creatures, loved only by their maker."* Opposite: *Lichen on granite in the Sierra.*

creation subjected to the same laws of life as his subjects? Oh, all these things are satanic, or in some way connected with the first garden.

Now, it never seems to occur to these far-seeing teachers that Nature's object in making animals and plants might possibly be first of all the happiness of each one of them, not the creation of all for the happiness of one. Why should man value himself as more than a small part of the one great unit of creation? And what creature of all that the Lord has taken the pains to make is not essential to the completeness of that unit — the cosmos? The universe would be incomplete without man; but it would also be incomplete without the smallest transmicroscopic creature that dwells beyond our conceitful eyes and knowledge.

From the dust of the earth, from the common elementary fund, the Creator has made *Homo sapiens*. From the same material he has made every other creature, however noxious and insignificant to us. They are earth-born companions and our fellow mortals. The fearfully good, the orthodox, of this laborious patchwork of modern civilization cry "Heresy" on every one whose sympathies reach a single hair's breadth beyond the boundary epidermis of our own species. Not content with taking all of earth, they also claim the celestial country as the only ones who possess the kind of souls for which that imponderable empire was planned.

This star, our own good earth, made many a successful journey around the heavens ere man was made, and whole kingdoms of creatures enjoyed existence and returned to dust ere man appeared to claim them. After human beings have also played their part in Creation's plan, they too may disappear without any general

burning or extraordinary commotion whatever.

Plants are credited with but dim and uncertain sensation, and minerals with positively none at all. But why may not even a mineral arrangement of matter be endowed with sensation of a kind that we in our blind exclusive perfection can have no manner of communication with?

But I have wondered from my object. I stated a page or two back that man claimed the earth was made for him, and I was going to say that venomous beasts, thorny plants, and deadly diseases of certain parts of the earth prove that the whole world was not made for him. When an animal from a tropical climate is taken to high latitudes, it may perish of cold, and we say that such an animal was never intended for so severe a climate. But when man betakes himself to sickly parts of the tropics and perishes, he cannot see that he was never intended for such deadly climates. No, he will rather accuse the first mother of [being] the cause of the difficulty, though she may never have seen a fever district; or will consider it a providential chastisement for some self-invented form of sin.

Furthermore, all uneatable and uncivilizable animals, and all plants which carry prickles, are deplorable evils which, according to closet researches of clergy, required the cleansing chemistry of universal planetary combustion. But more than aught else mankind required burning, as being in great part wicked, and if that transmundane furnace can be so applied and regulated as to smelt and purify us into conformity with the rest of the terrestrial creation, then the tophetization of the erratic genus Homo were a consummation devoutly to be prayed for. But, glad to leave these ecclesiastical fires and blunders, I joyfully return to the immortal truth

"Not a pine, not a palm, in all this garden excels these stately grass plants in beauty of wind-waving gestures."

and immortal beauty of Nature.

A Thousand-Mile Walk to the Gulf

Poison oak or poison ivy (*Rhus diversiloba*), both as a bush and a scrambler up trees and rocks, is common throughout the foothills region up to a height of at least three thousand feet above the sea. . . . Like most other things not apparently useful to man, it has few friends, and the blind question, "Why was it made?" goes on and on with never a guess that first of all it might have been made for itself.

My First Summer in the Sierra

Poor creatures, loved only by their maker, they are timid and bashful . . . and though perhaps not possessed of much of that charity that suffers long and is kind, seldom, either by mistake or by mishap, do harm to any one.

Certainly they cause not the hundredth part of the pain and death that follow the footsteps of the admired Rocky Mountain trapper. Nevertheless, again and again, in season and out of season, the question comes up, "What are rattlesnakes good for?" As if nothing that does not obviously make for the benefit of man had any right to exist; as if our ways were God's ways.

Our National Parks

Not a pine, not a palm, in all this garden excels these stately grass plants in beauty of wind-waving gestures. Here are panicles that are one mass of refined purple; others that have flowers as yellow as ripe oranges, and stems polished and shining like steel wire. Some of the species are grouped in groves and thickets like trees, while others may be seen waving without any companions in sight. Some of them have wide-branching panicles like Kentucky oaks, others with a few tassels of spikelets drooping from a tall, leafless stem. But all of them are beautiful beyond the reach of language. I rejoice that God has "so clothed the grass of the field." How strangely we are blinded to beauty and color, form and motion, by comparative size! For example, we measure grasses by our own stature and by the height and bulkiness of trees. But what is the size of the greatest man, or the tallest tree that ever overtopped a grass! Compared with other things in God's creation the difference is nothing. We all are only microscopic animalcula.

A Thousand-Mile Walk to the Gulf

. . . Most of these meadows are now in their prime. How wonderful must be the temper of the elastic leaves of grasses and sedges to make curves so perfect and fine. Tempered a little harder, they would stand erect, stiff and bristly, like strips of metal; a little softer, and every leaf would lie flat. And what fine painting and tinting there is on the plumes and pales, stamens and feathery pistils. Butterflies colored like the flowers waver above them in wonderful profusion, and many other beautiful winged people, numbered and known and loved only by the Lord, are waltzing together high overhead, seemingly in pure play and hilarious enjoyment of their little sparks of life. How wonderful they are! How do they get a living, and endure the weather? How are their little bodies, with muscles, nerves, organs, kept warm and jolly in such admirable exuberant health? Regarded only as mechanical inventions, how wonderful they are! Compared with these, godlike man's greatest machines are as nothing.

My First Summer in the Sierra

Found a single specimen of a handsome little plant, which at once, in some mysterious way, brought to mind a young friend in Indiana. How wonderfully our thoughts and impressions are stored! There is that in the glance of a flower which may at times control the greatest of creation's braggard lords.

A Thousand-Mile Walk to the Gulf

. . . [S]hortly after sunrise, just as the light was beginning to come streaming through the trees, while I lay leaning on my elbow taking my bread and tea, and looking down across the cañon, tracing the dip of the granite headlands, and trying to plan a way to the river at a point likely to be fordable, suddenly I caught the big bright eyes of a deer gazing at me through the garden hedge. The expressive eyes, the slim black-tipped muzzle, and the large ears were as perfectly visible as if placed there at just the right distance to be seen, like a picture on a wall. She continued to gaze, while I gazed back with equal steadiness, motionless as a rock. In a few minutes she ventured forward a step, exposing her fine arching neck and forelegs, then snorted and withdrew.

This alone was a fine picture — the beautiful eyes framed in colored cherry leaves, the topmost sprays lightly atremble, and just glanced by the level sunrays, all the rest in shadow.

But more anon. Gaining confidence, and evidently piqued by curiosity, the trembling sprays indicated her return, and her head came into view; then another and another step, and she stood wholly exposed inside the garden hedge, gazed eagerly around, and again withdrew, but returned a moment afterward, this time advancing into the middle of the garden; and behind her I noticed a second pair of eyes, not fixed on me, but on her companion in front, as if eagerly questioning, "What in the world do you see?" Then more rustling in the hedge, and another head came slipping past the second, the two heads touching; while the first came within a few steps of me, walking with inimitable grace, expressed in every limb. My picture was being enriched and enlivened every minute; but even this was not all. After another timid little snort, as if testing my good intentions, all three disappeared; but I was true, and my wild beauties emerged once more, one, two, three, four, slipping through the dense hedge without snapping a twig, and all four came forward into the garden, grouping themselves most picturesquely, moving, changing, lifting their smooth polished limbs with charming grace — the perfect embodiment of poetic form and motion. I have oftentimes remarked in meeting with deer under various circumstances that curiosity was sufficiently strong to carry them dangerously near hunters; but in this instance they seemed to have satisfied curiosity, and began to feel so much at ease in my company that they all commenced feeding the garden — eating breakfast with me, like gentle sheep around a shepherd — while I observed keenly, to learn their gestures and what plants they fed on. They are the daintiest feeders I ever saw, and no wonder the Indians esteem the contents of their stomachs a great delicacy. They seldom eat grass, but chiefly aromatic shrubs. The ceanothus and cherry seemed their favorites. They would cull a single cherry leaf with the utmost delicacy, then one of ceanothus, now and then stalking across the garden to snip off a leaf or two of mint, their sharp muzzle enabling them to cull out the daintiest leaves one at a time. It was delightful to feel how perfectly the most timid wild animals may confide in man. They no longer required that I should remain motionless, taking no alarm when I shifted from one elbow to the other, and even allowed me to rise and stand erect.

It then occurred to me that I might possibly steal up to one of them and catch it, not with any intention of killing it, for that was far indeed from my thoughts. I only wanted to run my hand along its beautiful curving limbs. But no sooner had I made a little advance on this line than, giving a searching look, they seemed to penetrate my conceit, and bounded off with loud shrill snorts, vanishing in the forest . . . .

I have often tried to understand how so many deer, and wild sheep, and bears, and flocks of grouse — nature's cattle and poultry — could be allowed to run at large through the mountain gardens without in any way marring their beauty. I was therefore all the more watchful of this feeding flock, and carefully examined the garden after they left, to see what flowers had suffered; but I could not detect the slightest disorder, much less destruction. It seemed rather that, like gardeners, they had been keeping it in order. At least I could not see a crushed flower, nor a single grass stem that was misbent or broken down. Nor among the daisy, gentian, bryanthus gardens of the Alps, where the wild sheep roam at will, have I ever noticed the effects of destructive feeding or trampling. Even the burly shuffling bears beautify the ground on which they walk, picturing it with their awe-inspiring tracks, and also writing poetry on the soft sequoia bark in boldly drawn gothic hieroglyphics. But, strange to say, man, the crown, the sequoia of nature, brings confusion with all his best gifts, and, with the overabundant, misbegotten animals that he breeds, sweeps away the beauty of wildness like a fire.

"The New Sequoia Forests of California,"
Harper's Monthly, November 1878

Lizards of every temper, style, and color dwell here, seemingly as happy and companionable as the birds and squirrels. Lowly, gentle fellow mortals, enjoying God's sunshine, and doing the best they can in getting a living, I like to watch them at their work and play. They bear acquaintance well, and one likes them the better the longer one looks into their beautiful, innocent eyes. They are easily tamed, and one soons learns to love them, as they dart about on the hot rocks, swift as dragon-flies. The eye can hardly follow them; but they never make long-sustained runs, usually only about ten or twelve feet, then a sudden stop, and as sudden a start again; going all their journeys by quick, jerking impulses. These many stops I find are necessary as rests, for they are short-winded, and when pursued steadily are soon out of breath, pant pitifully, and are easily caught. Their bodies are more than half tail, but these tails are well managed, never heavily dragged nor curved up as if hard to carry; on the contrary, they seem to follow the body lightly of their own will. Some are colored like the sky, bright as bluebirds, others gray like the lichened rocks on which they hunt and bask. Even the horned toad of the plains is a mild, harmless creature, and so are the snake-like species which glide in curves with true snake motion, while their small, undeveloped limbs drag as useless appendages. One specimen fourteen inches long which I observed closely made no use whatever of its tender,

sprouting limbs, but glided with all the soft, sly ease and grace of a snake. Here comes a little, gray, dusty fellow who seems to know and trust me, running about my feet, and looking up cunningly into my face. Carlo is watching, makes a quick pounce on him, for the fun of the thing I suppose; but Liz has shot away from his paws like an arrow, and is safe in the recesses of a clump of chaparral. Gentle saurians, dragons, descendants of an ancient and mighty race, Heaven bless you all and make your virtues known! for few of us know as yet that scales may cover fellow creatures as gentle and lovable as feathers, or hair, or cloth.

Mastodons and elephants used to live here no great geological time ago, as shown by their bones, often discovered by miners in washing gold-gravel. And bears of at least two species are here now, besides the California lion or panther, and wild cats, wolves, foxes, snakes, scorpions, wasps, tarantulas; but one is almost tempted at times to regard a small savage black ant as the master existence of this vast mountain world. These fearless, restless, wandering imps, though only about a quarter of an inch long, are fonder of fighting and biting than any beast I know. They attack every living thing around their homes, often without cause as far as I can see. Their bodies are mostly jaws curved like ice-hooks, and to get work for these weapons seems to be their chief aim and pleasure. Most of their colonies are established in living oaks somewhat decayed or hollowed, in which they can conveniently build their cells. These are chosen probably because of their strength as opposed to the attacks of animals and storms. They work both day and night, creep into dark caves, climb the highest trees, wander and hunt through cool ravines as well as on hot, unshaded ridges, and extend their highways and byways over everything but water and sky. From the foothills to a mile above the level of the sea nothing can stir without their knowledge; and alarms are spread in an incredibly

short time, without any howl or cry that we can hear. I can't understand the need of their ferocious courage; there seems to be no common sense in it. Sometimes, no doubt, they fight in defense of their homes, but they fight anywhere and always wherever they can find anything to bite. As soon as a vulnerable spot is discovered on man or beast, they stand on their heads and sink their jaws, and though torn limb from limb, they will yet hold on and die biting deeper. When I contemplate this fierce creature so widely distributed and strongly intrenched, I see that much remains to be done ere the world is brought under the rule of universal peace and love.

On my way to camp a few minutes ago, I passed a dead pine nearly ten feet in diameter. It has been enveloped in fire from top to bottom so that now it looks like a grand black pillar set up as a monument. In this noble shaft a colony of large jet-black ants have established themselves, laboriously cutting tunnels and cells through the wood, whether sound or decayed. The entire trunk seems to have been honeycombed, judging by the size of the talus of gnawed chips like sawdust piled up around its base. They are more intelligent looking than their small, belligerent, strong-scented brethren, and have better manners, though quick to fight when required. Their towns are carved in fallen trunks as well as in those left standing, but never in sound, living trees or in the ground. When you happen to sit down to rest or take notes near a colony, some wandering hunter is sure to find you and come cautiously forward to discover the nature of the intruder and what ought to be done. If you are not too near the town and keep perfectly still he may run across your feet a few times, over your legs and hands and face, up your trousers, as if taking your measure and getting comprehensive views, then go in peace without raising an alarm. If, however, a tempting spot is offered or some suspicious movements excites him, a bite follows, and such a bite! I fancy that a bear or wolf bite is not to be compared with it. A quick electric flame of pain flashes along the outraged nerves, and you discover for the first time how great is the capacity for sensation you are possessed of. A shriek, a grab for the animal, and a bewildered stare follow this bite of bites as one comes back to consciousness from sudden eclipse. Fortunately, if careful, one need not be bitten oftener than once or twice in a lifetime. This wonderful electric species is about three-fourths of an inch long. Bears are fond of them, and tear and gnaw their home-logs to pieces, and roughly devour the eggs, larvae, parent ants, and the rotten or sound wood of the cells, all in one spicy acid hash. The Digger Indians also are fond of the larvae and even of the perfect ants, so I have been told by old mountaineers. They bite off and reject the head, and eat the tickly acid body with keen relish. Thus are the poor biters bitten, like every other biter, big or little, in the world's great family.

There is also a fine, active, intelligent-looking red species, intermediate in size between the above. They dwell in the ground, and build large piles of seed husks, leaves, straw, etc., over their nest. Their food seems to be mostly insects and plant leaves, seeds and sap. How many mouths Nature has to fill, how many neighbors we have, and how seldom we get in each other's way! Then to think of the infinite numbers of smaller fellow mortals, invisibly small, compared with which the smallest ants are as mastodons.

My First Summer in the Sierra

Pearl cumuli over the higher mountains — clouds, not with a silver lining, but all silver. The brightest, crispest, rockiest-looking clouds, most varied in features and keenest in outline I ever saw at any time of year in any country. The daily building and unbuilding of these snowy cloud-ranges — the highest Sierra — is a prime marvel to me, and I gaze at the stupendous white domes, miles high, with ever fresh admiration. But in the midst of these sky and mountain affairs a change of diet is pulling us down. We have been out of bread a few days, and begin to miss it more than seems reasonable, for we have plenty of meat and sugar and tea. Strange we should feel food-poor in so rich a wilderness. The Indians put us to shame, so do the squirrels —

(continued on p. 136)

starchy roots and seeds and bark in abundance, yet the failure of the meal sack disturbs our bodily balance, and threatens our best enjoyments.

July 3 — Warm. Breeze just enough to sift through the woods and waft fragrance from their thousand fountains. The pine and fir cones are growing well, resin and balsam dripping from every tree, and seeds are ripening fast, promising a fine harvest. The squirrels will have bread. They eat all kinds of nuts long before they are ripe, and yet never seem to suffer in stomach.

July 4 — The air beyond the flock range, full of the essences of the woods, is growing sweeter and more fragrant from day to day, like ripening fruit.

Mr. Delaney is expected to arrive soon from the lowlands with a new stock of provisions, and as the flock is to be moved to fresh pastures we shall all be well fed. In the meantime our stock of beans as well as flour has failed — everything but mutton, sugar and tea. The shepherd is somewhat demoralized, and seems to care but little what becomes of his flock. He says that since the boss has failed to feed him he is not rightly bound to feed the sheep, and swears that no decent white man can climb these steep mountains on mutton alone. "It's not fittin' grub for a white man really white. For dogs and coyotes and Indians it's different. Good grub, good sheep. That's what I say." Such was Billy's Fourth of July oration.

July 5 — The clouds of noon on the High Sierra seem yet more marvelously, indescribably beautiful from day to day as one becomes more wakeful to see them. The smoke of the gunpowder burned yesterday on the lowlands, and the eloquence of the orators has probably settled or been blown away by this time. Here every day is a holiday, a jubilee ever sounding with serene enthusiasm, without wear or waste or cloying weariness. Everything rejoicing. Not a single cell or crystal unvisited or forgotten.

July 6 — Mr. Delaney has not arrived, and the bread famine is sore. We must eat mutton a while longer, though it seems hard to get accustomed to it. I have heard of Texas pioneers

Oak tree, Yosemite: a solitary invitation.

living without bread or anything made from cereals for months without suffering, using the breast-meat of wild turkeys for bread. Of this kind they had plenty in the good old days when life, though considered less safe, was fussed over the less. The trappers and fur traders of early days in the Rocky Mountain regions lived on bison and beaver meat for months. Salmon-eaters, too, there are among both Indians and whites who seem to suffer little or not at all from the want of bread. Just at this moment mutton seems the least desirable of food, though of good quality. We pick out the leanest bits, and down they go against heavy disgust, causing nausea and an effort to reject the offensive stuff. Tea

makes matters worse, if possible. The stomach begins to assert itself as an independent creature with a will of its own. We should boil lupine leaves, clover, starchy petioles, and saxifrage rootstocks like the Indians. We try to ignore our gastric troubles, rise and gaze about us, turn our eyes to the mountains, and climb doggedly up through brush and rocks into the heart of the scenery. A stifled calm comes on, and the day's duties and even enjoyments are languidly got through with. We chew a few leaves of ceanothus by way of luncheon, and smell or chew the spicy monardella for the dull headache and stomach-ache that now lightens, now comes muffling down upon us and into us like fog. At night more mutton, flesh to flesh, down with it, not too much,

and there are the stars shining through the cedar plumes and branches above our beds.

July 7 — Rather weak and sickish this morning, and all about a piece of bread. Can scarce command attention to my best studies, as if one couldn't take a few days' saunter in the godful woods without maintaining a base on a wheat-field and grist-mill. Like caged parrots we want a cracker, any of the hundred kinds — the remainder biscuit of a voyage around the world would answer well enough, nor would the wholesomeness of saleratus biscuit be questioned. Bread without flesh is a good diet, as on many botanical excursions I have proved. Tea also may easily be ignored. Just bread and water and delightful toil is all I need — not unreasonably much, yet one ought to be trained and tempered to enjoy life in these brave wilds in full independence of any particular kind of nourishment. That this may be accomplished is manifest, as far as bodily welfare is concerned, in the lives of people of other climes. The Eskimo, for example, gets a living far north of the wheat line, from oily seals and whales. Meat, berries, bitter weeds, and blubber, or only the last, for months at a time; and yet these people all around the frozen shores of our continent are said to be hearty, jolly, stout, and brave. We hear, too, of fish-eaters, carnivorous as spiders, yet well enough as far as stomachs are concerned, while we are so ridiculously helpless, making wry faces over our fare, looking sheepish in digestive distress amid rumbling, grumbling sounds that might well pass for smothered baas. We have a large supply of sugar, and this evening it occurred to me that these belligerent stomachs might possibly, like complaining children, be coaxed with candy. Accordingly the frying-pan was cleansed, and a lot of sugar cooked in it to a sort of wax, but this stuff only made matters worse.

Man seems to be the only animal whose food soils him, making necessary much washing and shield-like bibs and napkins. Moles living in the earth and eating slimy worms are yet as clean as seals or fishes, whose lives are one perpetual wash. And, as we have seen, the squirrels in these resiny woods keep themselves clean in

*In his trip from Indiana to the Gulf, Muir detected little change
from Kentucky to Tennessee compared to the differences in Georgia
and Florida.* Opposite: *Gray's Arch, Red River Gorge, Kentucky.*

some mysterious way; not a hair is sticky, though they handle the gummy cones, and glide about apparently without care. The birds, too, are clean, though they seem to make a good deal of fuss washing and cleaning their feathers. Certain flies and ants I see are in a fix, entangled and sealed up in the sugar-wax we threw away, like some of their ancestors in amber. Our stomachs, like tired muscles, are sore with long squirming. Once I was very hungry in the Bonaventure graveyard near Savannah, Georgia, having fasted for several days; then the empty stomach seemed to chafe in much the same way as now, and a somewhat similar tenderness and aching was produced, hard to bear, though the pain was not acute. We dream of bread, a sure sign we need it. Like the Indians, we ought to know how to get the starch out of fern and saxifrage stalks, lily bulbs, pine bark, etc. Our education has been sadly neglected for many generations. Wild rice would be good. I noticed a leersia in wet meadow edges, but the seeds are small. Acorns are not ripe, nor pine nuts, nor filberts. The inner bark of pine or spruce might be tried. Drank tea until half intoxicated. Man seems to crave a stimulant when anything extraordinary is going on, and this is the only one I use. Billy chews great quantities of tobacco, which I suppose helps to stupefy and moderate his misery. We look and listen for the Don every hour. How beautiful upon the mountains his big feet would be!

In the warm, hospitable Sierra, shepherds and mountain men in general, as far as I have seen, are easily satisfied as to food supplies and bedding. Most of them are heartily content to "rough it," ignoring Nature's fineness as bothersome or unmanly. The shepherd's bed is often only the bare ground and a pair of blankets, with a stone, a piece of wood, or a pack-saddle for a pillow. In choosing the spot, he shows less care than the dogs, for they usually deliberate before making up their minds in so important an affair, going from place to place, scraping away loose sticks and pebbles, and trying for comfort by making many changes, while the shepherd casts himself down anywhere, seemingly the least skilled of all rest seekers. His food, too, even when he has all he wants, is usually far from delicate, either in kind or cooking. Beans, bread of any sort, bacon, mutton, dried peaches, and sometimes potatoes and onions, make up his bill-of-fare, the two latter articles being regarded as luxuries on account of their weight as compared with the nourishment they contain; a half-sack or so of each may be put into the pack in setting out from the home ranch and in a few days they are done. Beans are the main standby, portable, wholesome, and capable of going far, besides being easily cooked, although curiously enough a great deal of mystery is supposed to lie about the bean-pot. No two cooks quite agree on the methods of making beans do their best, and, after petting and coaxing and nursing the savory mess — well oiled and mellowed with bacon boiled into the heart of it — the proud cook will ask, after dishing out a quart or two for trial, "Well, how do you like *my* beans?" as if by no possibility could they be like any other beans cooked in the same way, but must needs possess some special virtue of which he alone is master. Molasses, sugar, or pepper may be used to give desired flavors; or the first water may be poured off and a spoonful or two of ashes or soda added to dissolve or soften the skins more fully, according to various tastes and notions. But, like casks of wine, no two potfuls are exactly alike to every palate. Some are supposed to be spoiled by the moon, by some unlucky day, by the beans having been grown on soil not suitable; or the whole year may be to blame as not favorable for beans.

My First Summer in the Sierra

The blue, or dusky, grouse is . . . common here. . . . Able to live on pine and fir buds, they are forever independent in the matter of food, which troubles so many of us and controls our movements. Gladly, if I could, I would live forever on pine buds, however full of turpentine and pitch, for the sake of this grand independence. Just to think of our sufferings last month merely for grist-mill flour. Man seems to have more difficulty than any other of the Lord's creatures. For many in towns it is a consuming, life-long struggle; for others, the danger of com-

ing to want is so great, the deadly habit of endless hoarding for the future is formed, which smothers all real life, and is continued long after every reasonable need has been over-supplied.

My First Summer in the Sierra

October 15 — I am now in the hot gardens of the sun, where the palm meets the pine, longed and prayed for and often visited in dreams, and, though lonely tonight amid this multitude of strangers, strange plants, strange winds, blowing gently, whispering, cooing, in a language I never learned, and strange birds also, everything solid or spiritual full of influences that I never before felt, yet I thank the Lord with all my heart for His goodness in granting me admission to this magnificent realm.

October 16 — Last evening when I was in the trackless woods, the great mysterious night becoming more mysterious in the thickening darkness, I gave up hope of finding food or a house bed, and searched only for a dry spot on which to sleep safely. . . . I walked rapidly for hours in the wet, level woods, but not a foot of dry ground could I find. Hollow-voiced owls were calling without intermission. All manner of night sounds came from strange insects and beasts, one by one, or crowded together. All had a home but I. Jacob on the dry plains of Padan-aram, with a stone pillow, must have been comparatively happy.

A Thousand-Mile Walk to the Gulf

Happy nowadays is the tourist, with earth's wonders, new and old, spread invitingly open before him, and a host of able workers as his slaves making everything easy, padding plush about him, grading roads for him, eager like the Devil, to show him all the kingdoms of the world and their glory and foolishness, spiritualizing travel for him with lightning and steam, abolishing space and time and almost everything else. Little children and tender, pulpy people, as well as storm-seasoned explorers, may now go almost everywhere in smooth comfort, cross oceans and deserts, scarce accessible to fish and birds, and dragged by steel horses, go up high mountains, riding gloriously beneath starry showers of sparks, ascending like Elijah in a whirlwind and chariot of fire.

Steep Trails

Arriving by the Panama steamer, I stopped one day in San Francisco and then inquired for the nearest way out of town. "But where do you want to go?" asked the man to whom I had applied for this important information. "To any place that is wild," I said. This reply startled him. He seemed to fear I might be crazy, and therefore the sooner I was out of town the better, so he directed me to the Oakland ferry.

The Yosemite

Tell me what you will of the benefactions of city civilization, of the sweet security of streets

— all as part of the natural upgrowth of man towards the high destiny we hear so much of. I know that our bodies were made to thrive only in pure air, and the scenes in which pure air is found. If the death exhalations that brood the broad towns in which we so fondly compact ourselves were made visible, we should flee as from a plague. All are more or less sick; there is not a perfectly sane man in San Francisco.

John of the Mountains

Two thousand years ago our Saviour told Nicodemus that he did not know where the winds came from, nor where they were going. And now in this Golden Age, though we Gentiles know the birthplace of many a wind and also "whither it is going," yet we know about as little of winds in general as those Palestinian Jews, and our ignorance, despite the powers of science, can never be much less profound than it is at present.

The substance of the winds is too thin for human eyes, their written language is too difficult for human minds, and their spoken language mostly too faint for the ears. A mechanism is said to have been invented whereby the human organs of speech are made to write their own utterances. But without any extra mechanical contrivance, every speaker also writes as he speaks. All things in the creation of God register their own acts. The poet was mistaken when he said, "From the wing no scar the sky sustains." His eyes were simply too dim to see the scar. In sailing past Cuba I could see a fringe of foam along the coast, but could hear no sound of waves, simply because my ears could not hear wave-dashing at that distance. Yet every bit of spray was sounding in my ears.

The subject brings to mind a few recollections of the winds I heard in my late journey. In my walk from Indiana to the Gulf, earth and sky, plants and people, and all things changeable

Kent and Donna Dannen

Kent and Donna Dannen

Always reveling in plant glory, Muir was taken up with the "simplicity and mysterious complexity of detail."
Opposite, left: *Yellow lady-slipper orchid.* Center: *Rhododendrons.* Right: *Shooting star (three times life size).*

were constantly changing. Even in Kentucky nature and art have many a characteristic shibboleth. The people differ in language and in customs. Their architecture is generically different from that of their immediate neighbors on the north, not only in planters' mansions, but in barns and granaries and the cabins of the poor. But thousands of familiar flower faces looked from every hill and valley. I noted no difference in the sky, and the winds spoke the same things. I did not feel myself in a strange land.

In Tennessee my eyes rested upon the first mountain scenery I ever beheld. I was rising higher than ever before; strange trees were beginning to appear; alpine flowers and shrubs were meeting me at every step. But these

Cumberland Mountains were timbered with oak, and were not unlike Wisconsin hills piled upon each other, and the strange plants were like those that were not strange. The sky was changed only a little, and the winds not by a single detectible note. Therefore, neither was Tennessee a strange land.

But soon came changes thick and fast. After passing the mountainous corner of North Carolina and a little way into Georgia, I beheld from one of the last ridge-summits of the Alleghenies that vast, smooth, sandy slope that reaches from the mountains to the sea. It is wooded with dark, branchy pines which were all strangers to me. Here the grasses, which are an earth-covering at the North, grow wide apart in tall clumps and tufts like saplings. My known flower companions were leaving me now, not one by one as in Kentucky and Tennessee, but in whole tribes and genera, and companies of shining strangers came trooping upon me in countless ranks. The sky, too, was changed, and I could detect strange sounds in the winds. Now I began to feel myself "a stranger in a strange land."

But in Florida came the greatest change of all, for here grows the palmetto, and here blow the winds so strangely toned by them. These palms and these winds severed the last strands of the cord that united me with home. Now I was a stranger, indeed. I was delighted, astonished, confounded, and gazed in wonderment blank and overwhelming as if I had fallen upon another star. But in all of this long, complex series of changes, one of the greatest, and the last of all, was the change I found in the tone and language of the winds. They no longer came with the old home music gathered from open prairies and waving fields of oak, but they passed over many a strange string. The leaves of magnolia, smooth like polished steel, the immense inverted forests of tillandsia banks, and the princely crowns of palms — upon these the winds made strange music, and at the coming-on of night had over-whelming power to present the distance from friends and home, and the completeness of my isolation from all things familiar.

Elsewhere I have already noted that when I was a day's journey from the Gulf, a wind blew upon me from the sea — the first sea breeze that had touched me in twenty years. I was plodding along with my satchel and plants, leaning weari-ly forward, a little sore from approaching fever, when suddenly I felt the salt air, and before I had time to think, a whole flood of long-dormant associations rolled in upon me. The Firth of Forth, the Bass Rock, Dunbar Castle, and the winds and rocks and hills came upon the wings of that wind, and stood in as clear and sudden light as a landscape flashed upon the view by a blaze of lightning in a dark night.

I like to cling to a small chip of a ship like ours when the sea is rough, and long, comet-tailed streamers are blowing from the curled top of every wave. A big vessel responds awkwardly with mixed gestures to several waves at once, lumbering along like a loose floating island. But our little schooner, buoyant as a gull, glides up one side and down the other of each wave hill in delightful rhythm. As we advanced the scenery increased in grandeur and beauty. The waves heaved higher and grew wider, with correspond-ing motion. It was delightful to ride over this unsullied country of ever-changing water, and when looking upward from the shallow vales, or abroad over the round expanse from the tops of the wave hills, I almost forgot at times that the glassy, treeless country was forbidden to walk-ers. How delightful it would be to ramble over it on foot, enjoying the transparent crystal ground, and the music of its rising and falling hillocks, unmarred by the ropes and spars of a ship; to study the plants of these waving plains and their stream-currents; to sleep in wild weather in a bed of phosphorescent wave-foam, or briny scented seaweeds; to see the fishes by night in pathways of phosphorescent light; to walk the glassy plain in calm, with birds and flocks of glittering flying fishes here and there, or by night with every star pictured in its bosom!

But even of the land only a small portion is free to man, and if he, among other journeys on forbidden paths, ventures among the ice lands and hot lands, or up in the air in balloon bubbles, or on the ocean in ships, or down into it a little way in smothering diving-bells — in all such small adventures man is admonished and often punished in ways which clearly show him that he is in places for which, to use an approved phrase, he was never designed. However, in view of the rapid advancement of our time, no one can tell how far our star may finally be subdued to man's will. At all events I enjoyed this drifting locomotion to some extent.

A Thousand-Mile Walk to the Gulf

How smooth and changeless seems the surface of the mountains about us! Scarce a track is to be found beyond the range of the sheep except on small open spots on the sides of the streams, or where the forest carpets are thin or wanting. On the smoothest of these open strips and patches deer tracks may be seen, and the great

suggestive footprints of bears, which, with those of the many small animals, are scarce enough to answer as a kind of light ornamental stitching or embroidery. Along the main ridges and larger branches of the river Indian trails may be traced, but they are not nearly as distinct as one would expect to find them. How many centuries Indians have roamed these woods nobody knows, probably a great many, extending far beyond the time that Columbus touched our shores, and it seems strange that heavier marks have not been made. Indians walk softly and hurt the landscape hardly more than the birds and squirrels, and their brush and bark huts last hardly longer than those of wood rats, while their more enduring monuments, excepting those wrought on the forests by the fires they made to improve their hunting grounds, vanish in a few centuries.

How different are most of those of the white man, especially on the lower gold region — roads blasted in solid rock, wild streams dammed and tamed and turned out of their channels and led along the sides of cañons and valleys to work in mines like slaves. Crossing from ridge to ridge, high in the air, on long straddling trestles as if flowing on stilts, or down and up across valleys and hills, imprisoned in iron pipes to strike and wash away hills and miles of the skin of the mountain's face, riddling, stripping every gold gully and flat. These are the white man's marks made in a few feverish years, to say nothing of mills, fields, villages, scattered hundreds of miles along the flank of the Range. Long will it be ere these marks are effaced, though Nature is doing what she can, replanting, gar-

dening, sweeping away old dams and flumes, leveling gravel and boulder piles, patiently trying to heal every raw scar. The main gold storm is over. Calm enough are the gray old miners scratching a bare living in waste diggings here and there. Thundering underground blasting is still going on to feed the pounding quartz mills, but their influence on the landscape is light as compared with that of the pick-and-shovel storms waged a few years ago. Fortunately for Sierra scenery the gold-bearing slates are mostly restricted to the foothills. The region about our camp is still wild, and higher lies the snow about as trackless as the sky.

My First Summer in the Sierra

All of the Merced streams are wonderful singers, and Yosemite is the center where the main tributaries meet. From a point about half a mile from our camp we can see into the lower end of the famous valley, with its wonderful cliffs and groves, a grand page of mountain manuscript that I would gladly give my life to be able to read. How vast it seems, how short human life when we happen to think of it, and how little we may learn, however hard we try! Yet why bewail our poor inevitable ignorance? Some of the external beauty is always in sight, enough to keep every fibre of us tingling, and thus we are able to gloriously enjoy though the methods of its creation may lie beyond our ken. Sing on, brave Tamarack Creek, fresh from your snowy fountains, plash and swirl and dance to your fate in the sea; bathing, cheering every living thing along your way.

My First Summer in the Sierra

Baptism of Light

Perhaps it was his temporary blindness in 1867 that made John Muir so appreciative of light. He was using a sharp file to pull the lacing from a loose belt on a machine, when the file slipped and pierced his right eye. Soon both eyes were blind from sympathetic shock. Although the injured eye never fully recovered, the other one did, and both served him well through the rest of his long life.

These eyes saw much that other men missed. They were the eyes of an artist, and Muir often led landscape painters to inspiring vantage points in the Western mountains. Muir himself did field sketches, some of which were used to illustrate his books and articles. He saw how changes of light radically affected the beauty of a scene. Often refusing to carry even a blanket on his long wilderness treks, he was amused by photographers who weighed themselves down with cameras in the mountains. But his understanding of light, together with his close attention to detail and enthusiasm for hard work in difficult, even dangerous, situations, could have made Muir a great photographer.

Light, however, held even greater significance for Muir than for the artist. Light was a divine substance which flowed over and through creation to reveal God. It was a power beyond description or representation of which color, indeed all visual perception, was only subsidiary. As in the Gospel of John, light was to John Muir an analogy for God and even something more than analogy.

Opposite: *Muir was acutely aware of how changes of light drastically affected the beauty of a scene.*

Mighty as [a glacier's] effects appear to us, it has only developed the predestined forms of mountain beauty which were ready and waiting to receive the baptism of light.

Studies in the Sierra

[T]he day was divine and there was plenty of natural religion in the newborn landscapes that were being baptized in sunshine, and sermons in the glacial boulders on the beach where we landed.

Travels in Alaska

I do not like the doctrine of close communion as held by hard-shells, because the whole clumsy structure of the thing rests upon a foundation of coarse-grained dogmatism. Imperious, bolt-upright exclusiveness upon any subject is hateful, but it becomes absolutely hideous and impious in matters of religion, where all men are equally interested. I have no patience at all for the man who complacently wipes his pious lips and waves me away from a simple rite which commemorates the love and sacrifice of Christ, telling me, "Go out from us for you are not of us," and all this not for want of Christian love on my part, or the practice of self-denying virtues in seeking to elevate myself; but simply because in his infallible judgment I am mistaken in the number of quarts of that common liquid we call water which should be made use of in baptism.

I think infant baptism by sprinkling or any other mode is a beautiful and impressive ordinance, and however the Scripture of the thing is interpreted no parent can be doing an unseemly or un-Christian act in dedicating a child to God and taking upon him vows to lead his child in the path that all good people believe in. The baptism of an old sinner is apt to do but little good, but the baptism of an infant, in connection with the religious training which is supposed to follow it, is likely to do very much good.

I was baptized three times this morning. 1st (according to the old way of dividing the sermon), in balmy sunshine that penetrated to my very soul, warming all the faculties of spirit as well as the joints and marrow of body; 2nd, in the mysterious rays of beauty that emanate from plant corollas; and 3rd, in the spray of the lower Yosemite Falls. My 1st baptism was by immersion, the 2nd by pouring, and the 3rd by sprinkling. Consequently all Baptists are my bretheren, and all will allow that I've "got religion."

Letter to his brother David
April 10, 1870

[S]urprising effects are produced where the sunshine falls direct on rocky slopes and reverberates among boulders.

Our National Parks

All the wilderness seems to be full of tricks and plans to drive and draw us up into God's light.

My First Summer in the Sierra

Benevolent, solemn, fateful, pervaded with divine light, every landscape glows like a countenance hallowed in eternal repose; and every one of its living creatures, clad in flesh and leaves, and every crystal of its rocks, whether on the surface shining in the sun or buried miles deep in what we call darkness, is throbbing and pulsing with the heartbeats of God.

Our National Parks

But though in that terrible darkness I died to light, I lived again, and God who is the Light has led me tenderly from light to light to the shoreless ocean of rayless, beamless Spirit Light that bathes these holy mountains.

Letter to Mrs. Kate H. Daggett
December 1872

And what light has filled me since that time, I am sure you will be glad to know — the richest sun-gold flooding these California valleys, the spiritual alpenglow steeping the high peaks, silver light on the sea, the white glancing sun-spangles on rivers and lakes, light on the myriad stars of the snow, light sifting through the angles of sun-beaten icebergs, light in glacier caves, irised spray wafting from white waterfalls, and the light of calm starry nights beheld from mountain-tops dipping deep into the clear air. Aye, my lassie, it is a blessed thing to go free in

"Sunshine falls direct on rocky slopes and reverberates among boulders."

the light of this beautiful world, to see God playing upon everything, as a man would play on an instrument, His fingers upon the lightning and torrent, on every wave of sea and sky, and every living thing, making all together sing and shine in sweet accord, the one love-harmony of the Universe.

Letter to Miss Janet Douglas Moores
February 1887

Twenty Hill Hollow . . . may easily be visited by tourists *en route* for Yosemite, as it is distant only about six miles from Snelling's. . . . If you wish to see how much of light, life, and joy can be got into a January, go to this blessed Hollow. If you wish to see a plant-resurrection — myriads of bright flowers crowding from the ground, like souls to a judgment — go to Twenty Hills in February. If you are traveling for health, play truant to doctors and friends, fill your pocket with biscuits, and hide in the hills of the Hollow, lave in its waters, tan in its golds, bask in its flower-shine, and your baptisms will make you a new creature indeed. Or, choked in the sediments of society, so tired of the world, here will your hard doubts disappear, your carnal incrustations melt off, and your soul breathe deep and free in God's shoreless atmosphere of beauty and love.

Never shall I forget my baptism in this font. It happened in January, a resurrection day for

149

Opposite: *"California is the Golden State — in metallic gold, in sun gold, and in plant gold."*

Above: *Tioga Lake, High Sierra.* Overleaf: *Sunrise reflections of Mt. Hood on Lost Lake in Oregon.*
David Muench

many a plant and for me. I suddenly found myself on one of its hills; the Hollow overflowed with light, as a fountain, and only small, sunless nooks were kept for mosseries and ferneries. Hollow Creek spangled and mazed like a river. The ground steamed with fragrance. Light, of unspeakable richness, was brooding the flowers. Truly, said I, is California the Golden State — in metallic gold, in sun gold, and in plant gold. The sunshine for a whole summer seemed condensed into the chambers of that one glowing day. Every trace of dimness had been washed from the sky; the mountains were dusted and wiped clean with clouds — Pacheco Peak and Mount Diablo, and the waved blue wall between; the grand Sierra stood along the plain, colored in four horizontal bands: the lowest, rose purple; the next higher, dark purple; the next, blue; and, above all, the white row of summits pointing to the heavens.

It may be asked, What have mountains fifty, or a hundred miles away to do with Twenty Hill Hollow? To lovers of the wild, these mountains are not a hundred miles away. Their spiritual power and the goodness of the sky make them near, as a circle of friends. They rise as a portion of the hilled walls of the Hollow. You cannot feel yourself out of doors; plain, sky, and mountains ray beauty which you feel. You bathe in these spirit-beams, turning round and round, as if warming at a camp-fire. Presently you lose

consciousness of your own separate existence: you blend with the landscape, and become part and parcel of nature.

A Thousand-Mile Walk to the Gulf

There stood Mount Hood in all the glory of the alpenglow, looming immensely high, beaming with intelligence, and so impressive that one was overawed as if suddenly brought before some superior being newly arrived from the sky.

The atmosphere was somewhat hazy, but the mountain seemed neither near nor far. Its glaciers flashed in the divine light. The rugged, storm-worn ridges between them and the snow-fields of the summit, these perhaps might have been traced as far as they were in sight, and the blending zones of color about the base. But so profound was the general impression, partial analysis did not come into play. The whole mountain appeared as one glorious manifestation of divine power, enthusiastic and benevolent, flowing like a countenance with ineffable repose and beauty, before which we could only gaze in devout and lowly admiration.

Steep Trails

Now came the solemn, silent evening. Long, blue, spiky shadows crept out across the snow-fields, while a rosy glow, at first scarce discernible, gradually deepened and suffused every mountain-top, flushing the glaciers and the

(continued on p. 155)

151

David Muench

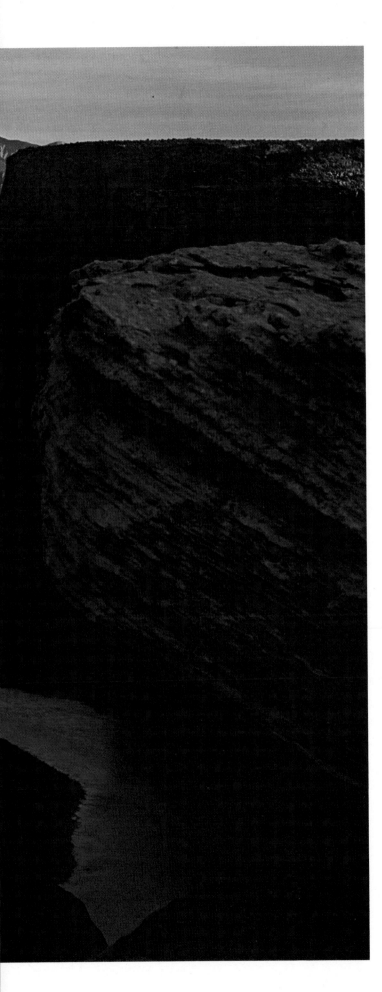

harsh crags above them. This was the alpenglow, to me one of the most impressive of all the terrestrial manifestations of God. At the touch of this divine light, the mountains seemed to kindle to a rapt, religious consciousness, and stood hushed and waiting like devout worshipers.

The Mountains of California

I wish you could see the holy morning alpenglow of Shasta.

Letter to Mrs. Ezra S. Carr
December 9, 1874

Beneath the frost shadows of the fiord we stood hushed and awe stricken, gazing at the holy vision; and had we seen the heavens opened and God made manifest, our attention could not have been more tremendously strained.... Peak after peak ... caught the heavenly glow, until all the mighty host stood transfigured, hushed and thoughtful, as if awaiting the coming of the Lord. The white, rayless light of morning, seen when I was alone amid the peaks of the California Sierra, had always seemed to me the most telling of all the terrestrial manifestations of God. But here the mountains themselves were made divine, and declared His glory in terms still more impressive. ... We turned and sailed away, joining the outgoing bergs, while "Gloria in excelsis" still seemed to be sounding over all the white landscape, and our burning hearts were ready for any fate, feeling that, whatever the future might have in store, the treasures we had gained this glorious morning would enrich our lives forever.

Travels in Alaska

[The Grand Canyon] is a vast wilderness of rocks in a sea of light, colored and glowing like oak and maple woods in autumn, when the sungold is richest.... But the *colors*, the living, rejoicing *colors*, chanting morning and evening in chorus to heaven! Whose brush or pencil, however lovingly inspired, can give us these?

Steep Trails

The dawn, as in all the pure, dry desert country is ineffably beautiful; and when the first

155

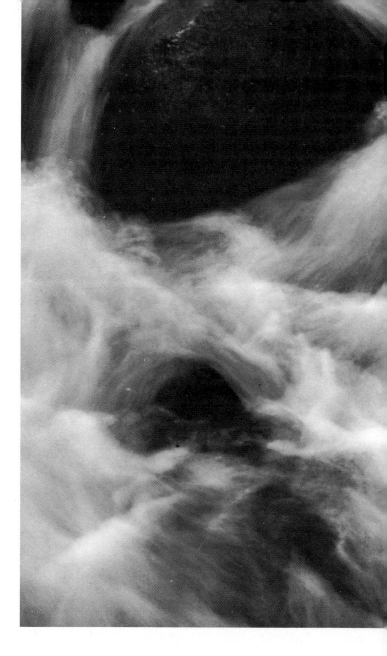

Light on rushing water patterns it into swirls of fog, into embryos of galaxies. Merced River.

level sunbeams sting the domes and spires, with what a burst of power the big, wild days begin! The dead and the living, rocks and hearts alike, awake and sing the new-old song of creation. All the massy headlands and salient angels of the walls, and the multitudinous temples and palaces, seem to catch the light at once, and cast thick black shadows athwart hollow and gorge, bringing out details as well as the main massive features of the architecture; while all the rocks, as if wild with life, throb and quiver and glow in the glorious sunburst, rejoicing. Every rock temple then becomes a temple of music; every spire and pinnacle an angel of light and song, shouting color hallelujahs.

As the day draws to a close, shadows, wondrous, black, and thick, like those of the morning, fill up the wall hollows. . . .Still deeper, richer, more divine grow the great walls and temples, until in the supreme flaming glory of sunset the whole cañon is transfigured, as if all the life and light of centuries of sunshine stored up and condensed in the rocks was now being poured forth as from one glorious fountain, flooding both earth and sky.

Steep Trails

At the bottom of the fall there is but little distinction of form visible. It is mostly a hissing, clashing, seething, upwhirling mass of scud and spray, through which the light sifts in gray and purple tones, while at times when the sun strikes at the required angle, the whole wild and apparently lawless, stormy, striving mass is changed to brilliant rainbow hues, manifesting finest harmony. . . . [I]n the boiling clouds of spray, there is no confusion, while the rainbow light makes all divine, adding glorious beauty and peace to glorious power.

The Yosemite

When I reached the foot of the fall sunbeams were glinting across its head, leaving all the rest in shadow; and on its illumined brow a group of yellow spangles of singular form and beauty were playing, flashing up and dancing in large flame-shaped masses, wavering at times, then steadying, rising and falling in accord with the

shifting forms of the water. But the color of the dancing spangles changed not at all. Nothing in clouds or flowers, on bird-wings or the lips of shells, could rival it in fineness. It was the most divinely beautiful mass of rejoicing yellow light I ever beheld — one of Nature's precious gifts that perchance may come to us but once in a lifetime.

The Yosemite

The Bridal Veil and Vernal Falls are famous for their rainbows; and special visits to them are often made when the sun shines into the spray at the most favorable angle. But amid the spray and foam and fine-ground mist ever rising from the various falls and cataracts there is an affluence and variety of iris bows scarcely known to visitors who stay only a day or two. Both day and night, winter and summer, this divine light

its sun fountain, cares not whether its passing light coins itself into other forms or goes unchanged.

Letter to Mrs. Ezra S. Carr
December 25, 1872

Every feature glowed with intention, reflecting the plans of God.

Travels in Alaska

[R]ocks and trees, everything alike drenched in gold light, heaven's colors coming down to the meadows and groves, making every leaf a romance, air, earth, and water in peace beyond thought, the great brooding days opening and closing in divine psalms of color.

Our National Parks

Now the sun rose, and filled the rocks with beamless spiritual light.

San Francisco Daily Evening Bulletin
August 24, 1875

Sunrise beams pouring through gaps in the rocky crest, warm level beams brushing across the shoulders in so fitting a way they seem to have worn channels for themselves as glaciers do. The oaks' stems are set aglow.

John of the Mountains

may be seen wherever water is falling, dancing, singing; telling the heart-peace of Nature amid the wildest displays of her power.

The Yosemite

[S]unshine streamed through the luminous fringes of the clouds and fell on the green waters of the fiord, the glittering bergs, and the crystal bluffs of the vast glacier, the intensely white, far-spreading fields of ice, and the ineffably chaste and spiritual heights of the Fairweather Range, which were now hidden, now partly revealed, the whole making a picture of icy wilderness unspeakably pure and sublime.

Travels in Alaska

Somehow, up here in these fountain skies I feel like a flake of glass through which light passes, but which, conscious of the inexhaustibleness of

. . . Innumerable insects begin to dance, the deer withdraw from the open glades and ridge-tops to their leafy hiding-places in the chaparral, the flowers open and straighten their petals as the dew vanishes, every pulse beats high, every life-cell rejoices, the very rocks seem to tingle with life, and God is felt brooding over everything great and small.

A dry spot a little way back from the margin of a silver fir lily garden makes a glorious camp-ground, especially where the slope is toward the east and opens a view of the distant peaks along the summit of the range. The tall lilies are brought forward in all their glory by the light of your blazing camp-fire, relieved against the outer darkness, and the nearest of the trees with their whorled branches tower above you like larger lilies, and the sky seen through the garden

157

Opposite: *The corn lily's striped leaves and lace flowers in Crescent Meadows, Sequoia National Park, are ringed by sequoias.*

opening seems one vast meadow of white lily stars.

In the morning everything is joyous and bright, the delicious purple of the dawn changes softly to daffodil yellow and white; while the sunbeams pouring through the passes between the peaks give a margin of gold to each of them. Then the spires of the firs in the hollows of the middle region catch the glow, and your camp grove is filled with light. The birds begin to stir, seeking sunny branches on the edge of the meadow for sun-baths after the cold night, and looking for their breakfasts, every one of them as fresh as a lily and as charmingly arrayed.

The Mountains of California

July 14 — How deathlike is sleep in this mountain air, and quick the awakening into newness of life! A calm dawn, yellow and purple, then floods of sun-gold, making everything tingle and glow.

My First Summer in the Sierra

On bright, crisp mornings a striking optical effect may frequently be observed from the shadows of the higher mountains while the sunbeams are pouring past overhead. Then every insect, no matter what may be its own proper color, burns white in the light. Gauzy-winged hymenoptera, moths, jet-black beetles, all are transfigured alike in pure, spiritual white, like snowflakes.

In this flowery wilderness the bees rove and revel, rejoicing in the bounty of the sun, clambering eagerly through bramble and huckle bloom, ringing the myriad bells of the manzanita, now humming aloft among polleny willows and firs, now down on the ashy ground among gilias and buttercups, and anon plunging deep into snowy banks of cherry and buckthorn. They consider the lilies and roll into them, and, like lilies, they toil not, for they are impelled by sunpower, as water-wheels by water-power; and when one has plenty of high-pressure water, the

other plenty of sunshine, they hum and quiver alike.

The Mountains of California

Looking eastward from the summit of the Pacheco Pass one shining morning, a landscape was displayed that after all my wanderings still appears as the most beautiful I have ever beheld. At my feet lay the Great Central Valley of California, level and flowery, like a lake of pure sunshine, forty or fifty miles wide, five hundred miles long, one rich furred garden of yellow compositae. And from the eastern boundary of this vast golden flower-bed rose the mighty Sierra, miles in height, and so gloriously colored and so radiant, it seemed not clothed with light, but wholly composed of it, like the wall of some celestial city. Along the top and extending a good way down, was a rich pearl-gray belt of snow; below it a belt of blue and dark purple, marking the extension of the forests; and stretching along the base of the range a broad belt of rose-purple; all these colors, from the blue sky to the yellow valley smoothly blending as they do in a rainbow, making a wall of light ineffably fine. Then it seemed to me that the Sierra should be called, not the Nevada or Snowy Range, but the Range of Light. And after ten years of wandering and wondering in the heart of it, rejoicing in its glorious floods of light, the white beams of the morning streaming through the passes, the noonday radiance on the crystal rocks, the flush of the alpenglow, and the irised spray of countless waterfalls, it still seems above all others the Range of Light.

The Yosemite

The greatest [snow] storms, however, are usually followed by a deep, peculiar silence, especially profound and solemn in the forests; and the noble trees stand hushed and motionless, as if under a spell, until the morning sunbeams begin to sift through their laden spires.

Our National Parks

At sundown the sombre crags and peaks were inspired with the ineffable beauty of the alpenglow, and a solemn, awful stillness hushed everything in the landscape. Then I crept into a hollow by the side of a small lake near the head of the cañon, smoothed a sheltered spot, and gathered a few pine tassels for a bed. After the short twilight began to fade I kindled a sunny fire, made a tin cupful of tea, and lay down to watch the stars. Soon the night-wind began to flow from the snowy peaks overhead, at first only a gentle breathing, then gaining strength, in less than an hour rumbled in massive volume something like a boisterous stream in a boulder-choked channel, roaring and moaning down the cañon as if the work it had to do was tremendously important and fateful; and mingled with these storm tones were those of the waterfalls on the north side of the cañon, now sounding distinctly, now smothered by the heavier cataracts of air, making a glorious psalm of savage wildness. My fire squirmed and struggled as if ill at ease, for though in a sheltered nook, detached masses of icy wind often fell like icebergs on top of it, scattering sparks and coals, so that I had to keep well back to avoid being burned. But the big resiny roots and knots of the dwarf pine could neither be beaten out nor blown away, and the flames, now rushing up in long lances, now flattened and twisted on the rocky ground, roared as if trying to tell the storm stories of the trees they belonged to, as the light given out was telling the story of the sunshine they had gathered in centuries of summers.

The stars shone clear in the strip of sky between the huge dark cliffs; and as I lay recalling the lessons of the day, suddenly the full moon looked down over the cañon wall, her face apparently filled with eager concern, which had a startling effect, as if she had left her place in the sky and had come down to gaze on me alone, like a person entering one's bedroom.

My First Summer in the Sierra

I witnessed one of the most glorious of our mountain sunsets; not one of the assembled mountains seemed remote — all had ceased their labor of beauty and gathered around their parent sun to receive the evening blessing, and waiting angels could not be more solemnly hushed. The sun himself seemed to have reached a

higher life as if he had died and only his soul were glowing with rayless, bodiless *Light,* and as Christ to his disciples, so this departing sun soul said to every precious beast, to every pine and weed, to every stream and mountain, "My peace I give unto you."

I ran home in the moonlight . . . down through the junipers, down through the firs, now in black shadow, now in white light, past great South Dome white as the moon, past spirit-like Nevada, past Pywiack, through the groves of Illilouette and spiry pines of the open valley, star crystals sparkling above, frost crystals beneath, and rays of spirit beaming everywhere.

I reached home a trifle weary, but could have wished so godful a walk some miles and hours longer, and . . . I said, "This is one of the big round ripe days that so fatten our lives — so much of sun on one side, so much of moon on the other."

Letter to Asa Gray,
December 18, 1872

[A]s I gazed every color seemed to deepen and glow as if the progress of the fresh sun-work were visible from hour to hour, while every tree seemed religious and conscious of the presence of God.

Our National Parks

The evening flames with purple and gold. The breeze that has been blowing from the lowlands dies away, and far and near the mighty host of trees baptized in the purple flood stand hushed and thoughtful, awaiting the sun's blessing and farewell — as impressive a ceremony as if it were never to rise again.

Our National Parks

The snowy skirts of the Wasatch Mountains appeared beneath the lifting fringes of the clouds, and the sun shone out through colored windows, producing one of the most glorious after-storm effects I ever witnessed. Looking across the Jordan, the gray sagey slopes from the base of the Oquirrh Mountains were covered with a thick, plush cloth of gold, soft and ethereal as a cloud, not merely tinted and gilded like

a rock with autumn sunshine, but deeply muffled beyond recognition. Surely nothing in heaven, nor any mansion of the Lord in all his worlds, could be more gloriously carpeted. Other portions of the plain were flushed with red and purple, and all the mountains and the clouds above them were painted in corresponding loveliness. Earth and sky, round and round the entire landscape, was one ravishing revelation of color, infinitely varied and interblended.

Steep Trails

The nearer peaks are perchance clad in sapphire blue, others far off in creamy white. In the broad glare of noon they seem to shrink and crouch to less than half their real stature, and grow dull and uncommunicative — mere dead, draggled heaps of waste ashes and stone, giving no hint of the multitude of animals enjoying life in their fastnesses, or of the bright bloom-bordered streams and lakes. But when storms blow they awake and arise, wearing robes of cloud and mist in majestic speaking attitudes like gods. In the color glory of morning and evening they become still more impressive; steeped in the divine light of the alpenglow their

earthiness disappears, and, blending with the heavens, they seem neither high nor low.

Our National Parks

Now comes the sundown. The west is all a glory of color transfiguring everything. Far up the Pilot Peak Ridge the radiant host of trees stand hushed and thoughtful, receiving the Sun's goodnight, as solemn and impressive a leave-taking as if sun and trees were to meet no more. The daylight fades, the color spell is broken, and the forest breathes free in the night breeze beneath the stars.

My First Summer in the Sierra

Only a few hills and domes of cloudland were built yesterday and none at all to-day. The light is peculiarly white and thin, though pleasantly warm. The serenity of this mountain weather in the spring, just when Nature's pulses are beating highest, is one of its greatest charms.

My First Summer in the Sierra

June 28 — Warm, mellow summer. The glowing sunbeams make every nerve tingle.

My First Summer in the Sierra

Toward the end of August the sunshine grows hazy, announcing the coming of Indian summer, the outlines of the landscapes are softened and mellowed, and more and more plainly are the mountains clothed with light, white-tinged with pale purple, richest in the morning and evening. The warm, brooding days are full of life and thoughts of life to come, ripening seeds with next summer in them or a hundred summers.

Our National Parks

. . . [H]ow glorious the shining after the short summer showers and after frosty nights when the morning sunbeams are pouring through the crystals on the grass and pine needles, and how ineffably spiritually fine is the morning-glow on the mountain-tops and the alpenglow of evening. Well may the Sierra be named, not the Snowy Range, but the Range of Light.

My First Summer in the Sierra

September 2 — A grand, red, rosy, crimson day — a perfect glory of a day. What it means I don't know. It is the first marked change from tranquil sunshine with purple mornings and evenings and still, white noons. There is nothing like a storm, however. The average cloudiness only about .08, and there is no sighing in the woods to betoken a big weather change. The sky was red in the morning and evening, the color not diffused like the ordinary purple glow, but loaded upon separate well-defined clouds that remained motionless, as if anchored around the jagged mountain-fenced horizon. A deep-red cap, bluffy around its sides, lingered a long time on Mt. Dana and Mt. Gibbs, drooping so low as to hide most of their bases, but leaving Dana's round summit free, which seemed to float separate and alone over the big crimson cloud. Mammoth Mountain to the south of Gibbs and Bloody Cañon, striped and spotted with snowbanks and clumps of dwarf pine, was also favored with a glorious crimson cap, in the making of which there was no trace of economy — a huge bossy pile colored with a perfect passion of crimson, that seemed important enough to be sent off to burn among the stars in majestic independence.

My First Summer in the Sierra

September 4 — All the vast sky is clear, filled only with mellow Indian summer light.

My First Summer in the Sierra

September 6 — Still another perfectly cloudless day, purple evening and morning, all the middle hours one mass of pure serene sunshine. Soon after sunrise the air grew warm, and there was no wind. One naturally halted to see what Nature intended to do. There is a suggestion of real Indian summer in the hushed, brooding, faintly hazy weather. The yellow atmosphere, though thin, is still plainly of the same general character as that of eastern Indian summer. The peculiar mellowness is perhaps in part caused by myriads of ripe spores adrift in the sky.

My First Summer in the Sierra

The forests we so admired in summer seem still more beautiful and sublime in this mellow autumn light. Lovely.

My First Summer in the Sierra

. . . [T]he eye is soon drawn. . .to revel in the glorious congregation of peaks on the axis of the range in their robes of snow and light.

My First Summer in the Sierra

Wonderful how completely everything in wild nature fits into us, as if truly part and parent of us. The sun shines not on but in us. The rivers flow not past, but through us, thrilling, tingling, vibrating every fiber and cell of the substance of our bodies, making them glide and sing. The trees wave and the flowers bloom in our bodies as well as our souls, and every bird song, wind song, and tremendous storm song of the rocks in the heart of the mountains is our song, our very own, and sings our love.

The song of God, sounding on forever. So pure and sure and universal is the harmony . . . as soon as we are absorbed in the harmony, plain, mountain, calm, storm, lilies and sequoias, forests and meads are only different strands of many-colored Light — are on the sunbeam!

John of the Mountains

163

God's
Own Temples

The wilderness was a temple to John Muir. Each day that he spent in it was a day of worship. It was in the wilds that God was most clearly revealed to him.

Muir may have gotten the temple image from William Cullen Bryant, who wrote "The groves were God's first temples." But Muir expanded the image to virtually every conceivable wilderness setting. Not only sequoia groves, but Yosemite mountains, the Grand Canyon, and Alaska ice flows were holy places of worship and revelation.

To Muir it seemed only logical that, since God himself had created these temples, he should be present more fully in them than in churches made by man. That cliffs or trees might be quarried or cut for materials to construct cathedrals seemed ironic to the naturalist who heard sermons in stones, to whom the trees were teachers of divine lessons. He did not deny the validity of man-made places of worship. But the superiority of natural temples was so apparent to him that all others seemed superfluous.

Today the golf course and weekend boating trip often are given artificial sanctification by those who feel the need to rationalize their absence from formal worship services. But Muir was totally sincere and faithful to his concept of the wilderness as a temple. His religious devotion called for daily rather than weekly worship. From his holy experiences in natural temples, he drew inspiration and a measure of God's own strength. When removed from wilderness sanctuaries, Muir felt distant from God.

Opposite: *"The groves were God's first temples."*

. . . In very foundational truth we had been in one of God's own temples and had seen Him and heard Him working and preaching like a man."
Travels in Alaska

After I had bathed in the bright river, sauntered over the meadows, conversed with the domes, and played with the pines, I still felt blurred and weary, as if tainted in some way with the sky of your streets. I determined, therefore, to run out for a while to say my prayers in the higher mountain temples. "The days are sinful," I said, "and, though now winter, no great danger need be encountered, and no sudden storm will block my return, if I am watchful."

Steep Trails

I am sitting here in a little shanty made of sugar pine shingles this Sabbath evening. I have not been at church a single time since leaving home. Yet this glorious valley might well be called a church, for every lover of the great Creator who comes within the broad overwhelming influence of the place fails not to worship as he never did before. The glory of the Lord is upon all his works; it is written plainly upon the fields of every clime, and upon every sky, but here in this place of surpassing glory the Lord has written in capitals. I hope that one day you will see and read with your own eyes.
Letter from Yosemite to his brother David, March 20, 1870

. . . [T]he Valley, comprehensively seen, looks like an immense hall or temple lighted from above.

But no temple made with hands can compare with Yosemite. Every rock in its walls seems to glow with life. Some lean back in majestic repose; others, absolutely sheer or nearly so for thousands of feet, advance beyond their companions in thoughtful attitudes, giving welcome to storms and calms alike, seemingly aware, yet heedless, of everything going on about them. Awful in stern, immovable majesty, how softly these rocks are adorned, and how fine and reassuring the company they keep: their feet among beautiful groves and meadows, their brows in the sky, a thousand flowers leaning confidingly against their feet, bathed in floods of water, floods of light, while the snow and waterfalls, the winds and avalanches and clouds shine and sing and wreathe about them as the years go by, and myriads of small winged creatures — birds, bees, butterflies — give glad animation and help to make all the air into music. Down through the middle of the Valley flows the crystal Merced, River of Mercy, peacefully quiet, reflecting lilies and trees and the onlooking rocks; things frail and fleeting and types of endurance meeting here and blending in countless forms, as if into this one mountain mansion Nature had gathered her choicest treasures, to draw her lovers into close and confiding communion with her.

The Yosemite

. . . [T]he wonderful mountain called Cathedral Peak is in sight. From every point of view it shows marked individuality. It is a majestic temple of one stone, hewn from the living rock, and adorned with spires and pinnacles in regular cathedral style. The dwarf pines on the roof look like mosses. I hope some time to climb to it to say my prayers and hear the stone sermons.
My First Summer in the Sierra

Every tree, every flower, every ripple and eddy of this lovely stream seemed solemnly to feel the presence of the great Creator. Lingered in this sanctuary a long time thanking the Lord with all my heart for His goodness in allowing me to enter and enjoy it.
A Thousand-Mile Walk to the Gulf

As if rubus and the grass leaf were not enough of God's tender prattle words of love, which we so much need in these mighty temples of power, yonder in the "benmost bore" are two blessed adiantums. Listen to them! How wholly infused with God is this one big word of love that we call the world!

Steep Trails

When I entered this sublime wilderness the day was nearly done, the trees with rosy, glow-

Opposite: *Well-named Cathedral Peak: "Almost conventional in form, . . .*
nobly adorned with spires and pinnacles, thrilling under floods
of sunshine . . . . " Above: *"Suncups" in the High Sierra.*

ing countenances seemed to be hushed and thoughtful, as if waiting in conscious religious dependence on the sun, and one naturally walked softly and awe-stricken among them. I wandered on, meeting nobler trees where all are noble, subdued in the general calm, as if in some vast hall pervaded by the deepest sanctities and solemnities that sway human souls. At sundown the trees seemed to cease their worship and breathe free.

Our National Parks

The sunbeams streaming through their feather arches brighten the ground, and you walk beneath the radiant ceiling in devout subdued mood, as if you were in a grand cathedral with mellow light sifting through colored windows, while the flowery pillared aisles open enchanting vistas in every direction.

Our National Parks

No feature, however, of all the noble landscape as seen from here seems more wonderful than the Cathedral itself, a temple displaying Nature's best masonry and sermons in stones.

. . .This I may say is the first time I have been at church in California, led there at last, every door graciously opened for the poor lonely worshiper. In our best times everything turns to religion, all the world seems a church and the mountains altars. . . .

My First Summer in the Sierra

Our world is indeed a beautiful one, and I was thinking, on going to church last Sabbath, that I would hardly accept of a free ticket to the moon or to Venus, or any other world, for fear that it might not be so good and so fraught with the glory of the Creator as our own.

Letter to Miss Emily Pelton,
May 23, 1865

July 24 — Clouds at noon occupying about half the sky gave half an hour of heavy rain to wash one of the cleanest landscapes in the world. How well it is washed! The sea is hardly less dusty than the ice-burnished pavements and ridges, domes and cañons, and summit peaks plashed with snow like waves with foam. How fresh the woods are and calm after the last films of clouds have been wiped from the sky! A few minutes ago every tree was excited, bowing to the roaring storm, waving, swirling, tossing their branches in glorious enthusiasm like worship. But though to the outer ear these trees are now silent, their songs never cease. Every hidden cell is throbbing with music and life, every fibre thrilling like harp strings, while incense is ever flowing from the balsam bells and leaves. No wonder the hills and groves were God's first temples, and the more they are cut down and hewn into cathedrals and churches, the farther off and dimmer seems the Lord himself. The same may be said of stone temples. Yonder, to the eastward of our camp grove, stands one of Nature's cathedrals, hewn from the living rock, almost conventional in form, about two thousand feet high, nobly adorned with spires and pinnacles, thrilling under floods of sunshine as if alive like a grove-temple, and well named "Cathedral Peak." Even Shepherd Billy turns at times to this wonderful mountain building, though apparently deaf to all stone sermons. Snow that refused to melt in fire would hardly be more wonderful than unchanging dullness in the rays of God's beauty. I have been trying to get him to walk to the brink of Yosemite for a view, offering to watch the sheep for a day, while he should enjoy what tourists come from all over the world to see. But though within a mile of the famous valley, he will not go to it even out of mere curiosity. "What," says he, "is Yosemite but a cañon — a lot of rocks — a hole in the ground — a place dangerous about falling into — a d—d good place to keep away from." "But think of the waterfalls, Billy — just think of that big stream we crossed the other day, falling half a mile through the air — think of that, and the sound it makes. You can hear it now like the roar of the sea." Thus I pressed Yosemite upon him like a missionary offering the gospel, but he would have none of it. "I should be afraid to look over so high a wall," he said. "It would make my head swim. There is nothing worth seeing anyway, only rocks, and I see plenty of them here. Tourists that spend their money to see rocks and falls are fools, that's all. You can't humbug me. I've been in this country too long for that."

Such souls, I suppose, are asleep, or smothered and befogged beneath mean pleasures and cares.

My First Summer in the Sierra

That new Yosemite valley is located in the heart of the Middle Fork Canyon, the most remote, and inaccessible, and one of the very grandest of all the mountain temples of the range. It is still sacred to Nature, its gardens untrodden, and every nook and rejoicing cataract wears the bloom and glad sun-beauty of primeval wildness. . . .

Letter to General John Bidwell,
December 3, 1877

We saw another party of Yosemite tourists today. Somehow most of these travelers seem to care but little for the glorious objects about them, though enough to spend time and money and endure long rides to see the famous valley. And when they are fairly within the mighty walls of the temple and hear the psalms of the falls, they will forget themselves and become devout. Blessed, indeed, should be every pilgrim in these holy mountains!

My First Summer in the Sierra

It seems strange that visitors to Yosemite should be so little influenced by its novel grandeur, as if their eyes were bandaged and their ears stopped. Most of those I saw yesterday were looking down as if wholly unconscious of anything going on about them, while the sublime rocks were trembling with the tones of the mighty chanting congregation of waters gathered from all the mountains round about, making music that might draw angels out of heaven. Yet respectable-looking, even wise-looking people were fixing bits of worms on bent pieces of wire to catch trout. Sport they called it. Should church-goers try to pass the time fishing in baptismal fonts while dull sermons were being preached, the so-called sport might not be so bad; but to play in the Yosemite temple, seeking pleasure in the pain of fishes struggling for their lives, while God himself is preaching his sublimest water and stone sermons!

My First Summer in the Sierra

The sunshine falls in glory through the colossal spires and crowns, each a symbol of health and strength, the noble shafts faithfully upright like the pillars of temples, upholding a roof of infinite leafy interlacing arches and fretted skylights.

Our National Parks

The Sierra Cathedral, to the south of camp, was overshadowed like Sinai. Never before noticed so fine a union of rock and cloud in form and color and substance, drawing earth and sky together as one; and so human is it, every feature and tint of color goes to one's heart, and we shout, exulting in wild enthusiasm as if all the divine show were our own. More and more, in a place like this, we feel ourselves part of wild Nature, kin to everything.

My First Summer in the Sierra

We found the shore lavishly adorned with a fresh arrival of assorted bergs that had been left stranded at high tide. They were arranged in a curving row, looking intensely clear and pure on the gray sand, and, with the sunbeams pouring through them, suggested the jewel-paved streets of the New Jerusalem.

Travels in Alaska

I must return to the mountains — to Yosemite. I am told that the winter storms there will not be easily borne, but I am bewitched, enchanted, and tomorrow I must start for the great temple to listen to the winter songs and sermons preached and sung only there.

Letter to Mrs. Ezra S. Carr,
November 15, 1869

One of these ancient flood boulders stands firm in the middle of the stream channel, just below the lower edge of the pool dam at the foot of the fall nearest our camp. It is a nearly cubical mass of granite about eight feet high, plushed with mosses over the top and down the sides to ordinary high-water mark. When I climbed on top of it today and lay down to rest, it seemed the most romantic spot I had yet found — the one big stone with its mossy level top and smooth sides standing square and firm and solitary, like an altar, the fall in front of it bathing it lightly with the finest of the spray, just enough to keep its moss cover fresh; the clear green pool beneath, with its foam-bells and its half circle of lilies leaning forward like a band of admirers, and flowering dogwood and alder trees leaning over all in sun-sifted arches. How soothingly, restfully cool it is beneath that leafy, translucent ceiling, and how delightful the water music — the deep bass tones of the fall, the clashing, ringing spray, and infinite variety of small low tones of the current gliding past the side of the boulder-island, and glinting against a thousand smaller stones down the ferny channel! All this shut in; every one of these influences acting at short range as if in a quiet room. The place seemed holy, where one might hope to see God.

After dark, when the camp was at rest, I groped my way back to the altar boulder and passed the night on it — above the water, beneath the leaves and stars — everything still more impressive than by day, the fall seen dimly white, singing Nature's old love song with solemn enthusiasm, while the stars peering through the leaf-roof seemed to join in the white water's song. Precious night, precious day to

abide in me forever. Thanks be to God for this immortal gift.

My First Summer in the Sierra

With inexpressible delight you wade out into the grassy sun-lake [a mountain meadow] feeling yourself contained in one of Nature's most sacred chambers, withdrawn from the sterner influences of the mountains, secure from all intrusion, secure from yourself, free in the universal beauty.

The Mountains of California

The making of gardens and parks goes on with civilization all over the world, and they increase both in size and number as their value is recognized. Everybody needs beauty as well as bread, places to play in and pray in, where nature may heal and cheer and give strength to body and soul alike. This natural beauty-hunger is made manifest . . . in our magnificent National Parks — the Yellowstone, Yosemite, Sequoia, etc. — Nature's sublime wonderlands, the admiration and joy of the world. Nevertheless, like anything else worthwhile, from the very beginning, however well guarded, they have always been subject to attack by despoiling gain-seekers and

mischief-makers of every degree from Satan to Senators, eagerly trying to make everything immediately and selfishly commercial, with schemes disguised in smug-smiling philanthropy, industriously, shampiously crying, "Conservation, conservation, panutilization," that man and beast may be fed and the dear Nation made great. Thus long ago a few enterprising merchants utilized the Jerusalem temple as a place of business instead of a place of prayer, changing money, buying and selling cattle and sheep and doves; and earlier still, the first forest reservation, including only one tree, was likewise despoiled. Ever since the establishment of the Yosemite National Park, strife has been going on around its borders and I suppose this will go on as part of the universal battle between right and wrong, however much its boundaries may be shorn, or its wild beauty destroyed.

The Yosemite

It appears, therefore, that Hetch Hetchy Valley, far from being a plain, common, rock-bound meadow, as many who have not seen it seem to suppose, is a grand landscape garden, one of Nature's rarest and most precious mountain temples. As in Yosemite, the sublime rocks

173

Aspen grove, North Rim of the Grand Canyon: part of a "grand landscape garden. . . ."

David Muench

of its walls seem to glow with life, whether leaning back in repose or standing erect in thoughtful attitudes, giving welcome to storms and calms alike, their brows in the sky, their feet set in the groves and gay flowerly meadows, while birds, bees, and butterflies help the river and waterfalls to stir all the air into music — things frail and fleeting and types of permanence meeting here and blending, just as they do in Yosemite, to draw her lovers into close and confiding communion with her.

The Yosemite

. . . I had told the beauty of Shadow Lake only to a few friends, fearing it might come to be trampled and "improved" like Yosemite. On my last visit, as I was sauntering along the shore on the strip of sand between the water and sod, reading the tracks of wild animals that live here, I was startled by a human track, which I at once saw belonged to some shepherd; for each step was turned out 35 degrees or 40 degrees from the general course pursued, and was also run over in an uncertain sprawling fashion at the heel, while a row of round dots on the right indicated the staff that shepherds carry. None but a shepherd could make such a track, and after tracing it a few minutes I began to fear that he might be seeking pasturage; for what else could he be seeking? Returning from the glaciers shortly afterward, my worst fears were realized. A trail had been made down the mountain-side from the north,

175

and all the gardens and meadows were destroyed by a horde of hoofed locusts, as if swept by a fire. The money-changers were in the temple.
The Mountains of California

[W]hat says the spirit about my final escape from Yosemite? You saw me at these rock altars years ago, and I think I shall remain among them. . . .
Letter to Mrs. Ezra S. Carr,
November 4, 1870

August 10 — Another of those charming exhilarating days that makes the blood dance and excites nerve currents that render one unweariable and well-nigh immortal. Had another view of the broad ice-ploughed divide, and gazed again and again at the Sierra temple and the great red mountains east of the meadows.
My First Summer in the Sierra

I am glad to know that you miss no opportunity in seeking Nature's altars. May she be good to you and feed your soul while you labor amid those Oakland wastes of civilization. . . .
Come to these purest of terrestrial fountains. Come and receive baptism and absolution from civilized sins. You were but sprinkled last year. Come and be immersed! You have never seen our Valley with her jewels on, never seen her flowers of snow.
Letter to J. B. McChesney,
December 10, 1872

. . .Frosty morning: Crystals grow in marvelous beauty and perfection of form these still nights, every one built as carefully as the grandest temple, as if planned to endure forever.
My First Summer in the Sierra

All day I have been gazing in growing admiration at the noble groups of the magnificent silver fir which more and more is taking the ground to itself. The woods above Crane Flat still continue comparatively open, letting in the sunshine on the brown needle-strewn ground. Not only are the individual trees admirable in symmetry and superb in foliage and port, but half a dozen or more often form temple groves in which the trees are so nicely graded in size and position as to seem one. Here, indeed, is the tree lover's paradise. The dullest eye in the world must surely be quickened by such a tree as these.
My First Summer in the Sierra

[T]he Secretary of the American Civic Association and the Sierra Club spoke on the highest value of wild parks as places of recreation, Nature's cathedrals, where all may gain inspiration and strength and get nearer to God.
Letter to Howard Palmer,
December 12, 1912

No other place has ever so overwhelmingly attracted me as this hospitable, godful wilderness.

My First Summer in the Sierra

Fountains
of Life

John Muir was a missionary. The purpose of his life was to carry the good news of wilderness revelation to all Americans. He desired that they might experience the presence of God that he felt in natural surroundings.

Muir began by preaching to everyone who would listen and some who would not. Then, under the constant urging of his friends, he began to write articles for newspapers and magazines in order to reach more people. Books followed, and the demand for his writing exceeded his ability to produce it. He never found the time to write all the books that were within him. A manuscript that he had been revising was on his bed when he died.

Of course, all missionary work would be futile if the natural temples were destroyed. Thus Muir launched a crusade to save the truly holy land. He felt that the preservation of "Nature's Bible" for the sake of the "fog-breathing public" could be accomplished best in national parks.

His book *Our National Parks,* from which all the quotations in this chapter are taken, describes the parks as they existed in Muir's time and some areas that had potential to become national parks. Such was his effectiveness, that even as he wrote the book Americans began to accept his good news. Their demand for more national parks necessitated footnotes acknowledging that some of the actions recommended in the book already had been carried out. Today the National Park System continues to expand, but not yet fast enough to accommodate the multitudes of Americans who seek in the parks for "fountains of life."

Opposite: *Dogwood in bloom, Yosemite Valley.*

Right: *Blue columbine.* Opposite: *Mary Lake in High Sierra, with Crystal Crag on far shore — a scene enjoyed by fishermen.*

The tendency nowadays to wander in wildernesses is delightful to see. Thousands of tired, nerve-shaken, over-civilized people are beginning to find out that going to the mountains is going home; that wildness is a necessity; and that mountain parks and reservations are useful not only as fountains of timber and irrigating rivers, but as fountains of life. Awakening from the stupefying effects of the vice of over-industry and the deadly apathy of luxury, they are trying as best they can to mix and enrich their own little ongoings with those of Nature, and to get rid of rust and disease. Briskly venturing and roaming, some are washing off sins and cobweb cares of the devil's spinning in all-day storms on mountains; sauntering in resiny pinewoods or in gentian meadow, brushing through chaparral, bending down and parting sweet, flowery sprays; tracing rivers to their sources, getting in touch with the nerves of Mother Earth; jumping from rock to rock, feeling the life of them, learning the songs of them, panting in whole-souled exercise, and rejoicing in deep, long-drawn breaths of pure wildness. This is fine and natural and full of promise.

[I]t is far safer to wander in God's woods than to travel on black highways or to stay at home.

As age comes on, one source of enjoyment after another is closed, but Nature's sources never fail. Like a generous host, she offers her brimming cups in endless variety, served in a grand hall, the sky its ceiling, the mountains its walls, decorated with glorious paintings and enlivened with bands of music ever playing. The petty discomforts that beset the awkward guest, the unskilled camper, are quickly forgotten, while all that is precious remains. Fears vanish as soon as one is fairly free in the wilderness.

Catching trout with a bit of bent wire is a rather trivial business, but fortunately people fish better than they know. In most cases it is the man who is caught. Trout-fishing regarded as bait for catching men, for the saving of both body and soul, is important, and deserves all the expense and care bestowed upon it.

To defrauded town toilers, parks in magazine articles are like pictures of bread to the hungry. I can write only hints to incite good wanderers to come to the feast.

Few in these hot, dim, strenuous times are quite sane or free; choked with care like clocks full of dust, laboriously doing so much good and making so much money — or so little — they are no longer good for themselves.

All the larger spaces were taken long ago; therefore most of the newcomers build their cabins where the beavers built theirs. They keep a few cows, laboriously widen their little meadow opening by hacking, girdling, and burning the rim of the close-pressing forest, and scratch and plant among the huge blackened logs and stumps, girdling and killing themselves in killing the trees.

[T]he wildest health and pleasure grounds accessible and available to tourists seeking escape from care and dust and early death are the parks and reservations of the West.

[I]f in the making of the West, Nature had what we call parks in mind — places for rest, inspiration, and prayers — this Rainier region must surely be one of them. In the centre of it there is a lonely mountain capped with ice; from the ice-cap glaciers radiate in every direction,

and young rivers from the glaciers; while its flanks, sweeping down in beautiful curves, are clad with forests and gardens, and filled with birds and animals. Specimens of the best of Nature's treasures have been lovingly gathered here and arranged in simple symmetrical beauty within regular bounds.

. . .The forests reach to a height of a little over six thousand feet, and above the forests there is a zone of the loveliest flowers, fifty miles in circuit and nearly two miles wide, so closely planted and luxuriant that it seems as if Nature, glad to make an open space between woods so dense and ice so deep, were economizing the precious ground, and trying to see how many of her darlings she can get together in one mountain wreath — daisies, anemones, geraniums, columbines, erythroniums, larkspurs, etc., among which we wade knee-deep and waist-deep, the bright corollas in myriads touching petal to petal. . . .Altogether this is the richest subalpine garden I ever found, a perfect floral elysium.

No matter how far you have wandered hitherto, or how many famous gorges and valleys you have seen, this one, the Grand Cañon of the Colorado, will seem as novel to you, as unearthly in the color and grandeur and quantity of its architecture, as if you had found it after death, on some other star; so incomparably lovely and grand and supreme is it above all the other cañons in our fire-moulded, earthquake-shaken, rain-washed, wave-washed, river and glacier sculptured world. It is about six thousand feet deep where you first see it, and from rim to rim ten to fifteen miles wide. Instead of being dependent for interest upon waterfalls, depth, wall sculpture, and beauty of parklike floor, like most other great cañons, it has no waterfalls in sight, and no appreciable floor spaces. The big river has just room enough to flow and roar obscurely, here and there groping its way as best it can, like a weary, murmuring, overladen traveler trying to escape from the tremendous, bewildering labyrinthic abyss, while its roar serves only to deepen the silence.

182

"Wildness is a necessity," whether it is the tremendous abyss of the Grand Canyon from Toroweap Overlook (opposite) or the regal pride of the eagle (right).

Instead of being filled with air, the vast space between the walls is crowded with Nature's grandest buildings — a sublime city of them, painted in every color, and adorned with richly fretted cornice and battlement spire and tower in endless variety of style and architecture. Every architectural invention of man has been anticipated, and far more, in this grandest of God's terrestrial cities.

The Yellowstone National Park . . . is a big, wholesome wilderness on the broad summit of the Rocky Mountains, favored with abundance of rain and snow — a place of fountains where the greatest of the American rivers make their rise. . . .
Beside the treasures common to most mountain regions that are wild and blessed with a kind climate, the park is full of exciting wonders. The wildest geysers in the world, in bright, triumphant bands, are dancing and singing in it amid thousands of boiling springs, beautiful and awful, their basins arrayed in gorgeous colors like gigantic flowers; and hot paint-pots, mud springs, mud volcanoes, mush and broth caldrons whose contents are of every color and consistency, plash and heave and roar in bewildering abundance. In the adjacent mountains, beneath the living trees the edges of petrified forests are exposed to view, like specimens on the shelves of a museum, standing on ledges tier above tier where they grew, solemnly silent in rigid crystalline of centuries ago, opening marvelous views back into the years and climates and life of the past. . . .

Fortunately, almost as soon as it was discovered it was dedicated and set apart for the benefit of the people, a piece of legislation that shines benignly amid the common dust-and-ashes history of the public domain. . . .
[Y]ou may take excursions whenever you like into the middle of the park, where the geysers and hot springs are reeking and spouting in their beautiful basins, displaying an exuberance of color and strange motion and energy admirably calculated to surprise and frighten, charm and shake up the least sensitive out of apathy into newness of life.
However orderly your excursions or aimless, again and again amid the calmest, stillest scenery you will be brought to a standstill hushed and awe stricken before phenomena wholly new to you. Boiling springs and huge deep pools of purest green and azure water, thousands of them, are plashing and heaving in these high, cool mountains as if a fierce furnace fire were burning beneath each one of them; and a hundred geysers, white torrents of boiling water and steam, like inverted waterfalls, are ever and anon rushing up out of the hot, black underworld. . . .
In these natural laboratories one needs stout faith to feel at ease. The ground sounds hollow underfoot, and the awful subterranean thunder shakes one's mind as the ground is shaken, especially at night in the pale moonlight, or when the sky is overcast with storm-clouds. In the solemn gloom, the geysers, dimly visible, look like monstrous dancing ghosts, and their wild songs and the earthquake thunder replying to the storms overhead seem doubly terrible, as

if divine government were at an end. But the trembling hills keep their places. The sky clears, the rosy dawn is reassuring, and up comes the sun like a god, pouring his faithful beams across the mountains and forest, lighting each peak and tree and ghastly geyser alike, and shining into the eyes of the reeking springs, clothing them with rainbow light, and dissolving the seeming chaos of darkness into varied forms of harmony. The ordinary work of the world goes on. Gladly we see flies dancing in the sunbeams, birds feeding their young, squirrels gathering nuts, and hear the blessed ouzel singing confidingly in the shallows of the river — most faithful evangel, calming every fear, reducing everything to love.

How admirable it is that, after passing through so many vicissitudes of frost and fire and flood, the physiognomy and even the complexion of the landscape should still be so divinely fine!

After this reviving experience, you should take a look into a few of the tertiary volumes of the grand geological library of the park, and see how God writes history.

In calm Indian summer, when the heavy winds are hushed, the vast forests covering hill and dale, rising and falling over the rough topography and vanishing in the distance, seem lifeless. No moving thing is seen as we climb the peaks, and only the low, mellow murmur of falling water is heard, which seems to thicken the silence. Nevertheless, how many hearts with warm red blood in them are beating under cover of the woods, and how many teeth and eyes are shining! A multitude of animal people, intimately related to us, but of whose lives we know almost nothing, are as busy about their own affairs as we are about ours: beavers are building and mending dams and huts for winter, and storing them with food; bears are studying winter quarters as they stand thoughtful in open spaces, while the gentle breeze ruffles the long hair on their backs; elk and deer, assembling on the heights, are considering cold pastures where

they will be farthest away from the wolves; squirrels and marmots are busily laying up provisions and lining their nests against coming frost and snow foreseen; and countless thousands of birds are forming parties and gathering their young about them for flight to the southlands; while butterflies and bees, apparently with no thought of hard times to come, and with countless other insect folk, are dancing and humming right merrily in the sunbeams and shaking all the air into music.

Wander here a whole summer, if you can. Thousands of God's wild blessings will search you and soak you as if you were a sponge, and the big days will go by uncounted. . . . The time will not be taken from the sum of your life. Instead of shortening, it will indefinitely lengthen it and make you truly immortal. Nevermore will time seem short or long, and cares will never again fall heavily on you, but gently and kindly as gifts from heaven.

The sun is setting; long, violet shadows are growing out over the woods from the mountains along the western rim of the park; the Absaroka range is baptized in the divine light of the alpenglow, and its rocks and trees are transfigured. Next to the light of the dawn on high mountain tops, the alpenglow is the most impressive of all the terrestrial manifestations of God.

Now comes the gloaming. The alpenglow is fading into earthy, murky gloom, but do not let your town habits draw you away to the hotel. Stay on this good fire-mountain and spend the night among the stars. Watch their glorious bloom until the dawn, and get one more baptism of light. Then, with fresh heart, go down to your work, and whatever your fate, under whatever ignorance or knowledge you may afterward chance to suffer, you will remember these fine, wild views, and look back with joy to your wanderings in the blessed old Yellowstone Wonderland.

A pair of golden eagles have made their home in Yosemite ever since I went there thirty years ago. Their nest is on the Nevada Fall Cliff,

184

opposite the Liberty Cap. Their screams are rather pleasant to hear in the vast gulfs between the granite cliffs, and they help the owls in keeping the echoes busy.

Not even genuine piety can make the robin-killer quite respectable. Saturday is the great slaughter day in the bay region. Then the city pot-hunters, with a rag-tag of boys, go forth to kill, kept in countenance by a sprinkling of regular sportsmen arrayed in self-conscious majesty and leggins, leading dogs and carrying hammerless, breech-loading guns of famous makers. Over the fine landscapes the killing goes forward with shameful enthusiasm. After escaping countless dangers, thousands fall, big bagfuls are gathered, many are left wounded to die slowly, no Red Cross Society to help them. Next day, Sunday, the blood and leggins vanish from the most devout of the bird-butchers, who go to church, carrying gold-headed canes instead of guns. After hymns, prayers, and sermon they go home to feast, to put God's song birds to use, put them in their dinners instead of in their hearts, eat them, and suck the pitiful little drumsticks. It is only race living on race, to be sure, but Christians singing Divine Love need not be driven to such straits while wheat and apples grow and the shops are full of dead cattle. Song birds for food! Compared with this, making kindlings of pianos and violins would be pious economy.

[T]he noble oaks and all these rock-shading, stream-embowering trees are as nothing amid the vast abounding billowy forests of conifers. During my first years in the Sierra I was ever calling on everybody within reach to admire them, but I found no one half warm enough until Emerson came. I had read his essays, and felt sure that of all men he would best interpret the sayings of these noble mountains and trees. Nor was my faith weakened when I met him in Yosemite. He seemed as serene as a sequoia. . .and forgetting his age, plans, duties, ties of every sort, I proposed an immeasurable camping trip back into the heart of the mountains. He seemed anxious to go, but consid-

erately mentioned his party. I said, "Never mind. The mountains are calling; run away, and let plans and parties and dragging lowland duties all 'gang tapsal-teerie.' We'll go up a cañon singing your own song. 'Good-by, proud world! I'm going home,' in divine earnest. Up there lies a new heaven and a new earth; let us go to the show." But alas, it was too late — too near the sundown of his life. The shadows were growing long, and he leaned on his friends. His party, full of indoor philosophy, failed to see the natural beauty and fullness of promise of my wild plan, and laughed at it in good-natured ignorance, as if it were necessarily amusing to imagine that Boston people might be led to accept Sierra manifestations of God at the price of rough camping. Anyhow, they would have none of it, and held Mr. Emerson to the hotels and trails.

After spending only five tourist days in Yosemite he was led away, but I saw him two days more; for I was kindly invited to go with the party as far as the Mariposa big trees. I told Mr. Emerson that I would gladly go to the sequoias with him, if he would camp in the grove. He consented heartily, and I felt sure that we would have at least one good wild memorable night around a sequoia camp-fire. Next day we rode through the magnificent forests of the Merced basin, and I kept calling his attention to the sugar pines, quoting his wood-notes, "Come listen what the pine tree saith," etc., pointing out the noblest as kings and high-priests, the most eloquent and commanding preachers of all the mountain forests, stretching forth their century-old arms in benediction over the worshipping congregations crowded about them. He gazed in devout admiration, saying but little, while his fine smile faded away.

Early in the afternoon, when we reached Clark's Station, I was surprised to see the party dismount. And when I asked if we were not going up into the grove to camp they said: "No; it would never do to lie out in the night air, Mr. Emerson might take cold; and you know, Mr. Muir, that would be a dreadful thing." In vain I urged, that only in homes and hotels were colds caught, that nobody ever was known to take cold

camping in these woods, that there was not a single cough or sneeze in all the Sierra. Then I pictured the big climate-changing, inspiring fire I would make, praised the beauty and fragrance of sequoia flame, and told how the great trees would stand about us transfigured in the purple light, while the stars looked down between the great domes; ending by urging them to come on and make an immortal Emerson night of it. But the house habit was not to be overcome, nor the strange dread of pure night air, though it is only cooled day air with a little dew in it. So the carpet dust and unknowable reeks were preferred. And to think of this being a Boston choice! Sad commentary on culture and the glorious transcendentalism.

Accustomed to reach whatever place I started for, I was going up the mountain alone to camp and wait the coming of the party next day. But since Emerson was so soon to vanish, I concluded to stop with him. He hardly spoke a word all the evening, yet it was a great pleasure simply to be near him, warming in the light of his face as at a fire. In the morning we rode up the trail through a noble forest of pine and fir into the famous Mariposa Grove, and stayed an hour or two, mostly in ordinary tourist fashion — looking at the biggest giants, measuring them with a tape line, riding through prostrate fire-bored trunks, etc., though Mr. Emerson was alone occasionally, sauntering about as if under a spell. As we walked through a fine group, he quoted, "There were giants in those days," recognizing the antiquity of the race. To commemorate his visit, Mr. Galen Clark, the guardian of the grove, selected the finest of the unnamed trees and requested him to give it a name. He named it Samoset, after the New England sachem, as the best that occurred to him.

The poor bit of measured time was soon spent, and while the saddles were being adjusted I again urged Emerson to stay. "You are yourself a sequoia," I said. "Stop and get acquainted with your big brethren." But he was past his prime, and was now a child in the hands of his affectionate but sadly civilized friends, who seemed as full of old-fashioned conformity as of

bold intellectual independence. It was the afternoon of the day and the afternoon of his life, and his course was now westward down all the mountains to the sunset. The party mounted and rode away in wondrous contentment, apparently, tracing the trail through ceanothus and dogwood bushes, around the bases of the big trees, up the slope of the sequoia basin, and over the divide. I followed to the edge of the grove. Emerson lingered in the rear of the train, and when he reached the top of the ridge, after all the rest of the party were over and out of sight, he turned his horse, took off his hat and waved me a last good-by. I felt lonely, so sure had I been that Emerson of all men would be the quickest to see the mountains and sing them. Gazing awhile on the spot where he vanished, I

sauntered back into the heart of the grove, made
a bed of sequoia plumes and ferns by the side of
a stream, gathered a store of firewood, and then
walked about until sundown. The birds, robins,
thrushes, warblers, etc., that had kept out of
sight, came about me, now that all was quiet,
and made cheer. After sundown I built a great
fire, and as usual had it all to myself. And
though lonesome for the first time in these
forests, I quickly took heart again — the trees
had not gone to Boston, nor the birds; and as I
sat by the fire, Emerson was still with me in
spirit, though I never again saw him in the flesh.
He sent books and wrote, cheering me on;
advised me not to stay too long in solitude. Soon
he hoped that my guardian angel would intimate
that my probation was at a close. Then I was to
roll up my herbariums, sketches, and poems
(though I never knew I had any poems), and
come to his house; and when I tired of him and
his humble surroundings, he would show me to
better people.

But there remained many a forest to wander
through, many a mountain and glacier to cross,
before I was to see his Wachusett and Monad-
nock, Boston and Concord. It was seventeen
years after our parting on the Wawona ridge
that I stood beside his grave under a pine tree
on the hill above Sleepy Hollow. He had gone to
higher Sierras, and, as I fancied, was again
waving his hand in friendly recognition.

One touch of nature makes the whole world
kin. . . .

None of Nature's landscapes are ugly so long
as they are wild; and much, we can say comfort-
ingly, must always be in the great part wild,
particularly the sea and the sky, the floods of
light from the stars, and the warm, unspoilable
heart of the earth, infinitely beautiful, though
only dimly visible to the eye of imagination. The
geysers, too, spouting from the hot underworld;
the steady, long-lasting glaciers on the mountains, obedient only to the sun; Yosemite domes
and the tremendous grandeur of rocky cañons
and mountains in general — these must always
be wild, for man can change them and mar them
hardly more than can the butterflies that hover
above them. But the continent's outer beauty is
fast passing away, especially the plant part of it,
the most destructible and the most universally
charming of all.

In their natural condition, or under wise man-
agement, keeping out destructive sheep, pre-

venting fires, selecting the trees that should be
cut for lumber, and preserving the young ones
and the shrubs and sod of herbaceous vegetation, these forests would be a never failing
fountain of wealth and beauty. The cool shades
of the forest give rise to moist beds and currents
of air, and the sod of grasses and the various
flowering plants and shrubs thus fostered, together with the network and sponge of tree
roots, absorb and hold back the rain and the
waters from melting snow, compelling them to
ooze and percolate and flow gently through the
soil in streams that never dry. All the pine
needles and rootlets and blades of grass, and the
fallen, decaying trunks of trees, are dams, storing the bounty of the clouds and dispensing it in
perennial life-giving streams, instead of allowing
it to gather suddenly and rush headlong in short-
lived devastating floods. Everybody on the dry
side of the continent is beginning to find this out,
and, in view of the waste going on, is growing

more and more anxious for government protection. The outcries we hear against forest reservations come mostly from thieves who are wealthy and steal timber by wholesale. They have so long been allowed to steal and destroy in peace that any impediment to forest robbery is denounced as a cruel and irreligious interference with "vested rights," likely to endanger the repose of all ungodly welfare. . . .

Even in Congress a sizable chunk of gold, carefully concealed, will outtalk and outfight all the nation on a subject like forestry, well smothered in ignorance, and in which the money interests of only a few are conspicuously involved. Under these circumstances, the bawling, blethering oratorical stuff drowns the voice of God himself. Yet the dawn of a new day in forestry is breaking. Honest citizens see that only the rights of the government are being trampled, not those of the settlers. Only what belongs to all alike is reserved, and every acre that is left should be held together under the federal government as a basis for a general policy of administration for the public good. The people will not always be deceived by selfish opposition, whether from lumber and mining corporations or from sheepmen and prospectors, however cunningly brought forward underneath fables and gold.

Emerson says that things refuse to be mismanaged long. An exception would seem to be found in the case of our forests, which have been mismanaged rather long, and now come desperately near being like smashed eggs and spilt milk. Still, in the long run the world does not move backward. The wonderful advance made in the last few years, in creating four national parks in the West, and thirty forest reservations, embracing nearly forty million acres; and in the planting of the borders of streets and highways and spacious parks in all the great cities, to satisfy the natural taste and hunger for landscape beauty and righteousness that God has put, in some measure, into every human being and animal, shows the trend of awakening public

opinion. The making of the far-famed New York Central Park was opposed by even good men, with misguided pluck, perseverance, and ingenuity; but straight right won its way, and now that park is appreciated. So we confidently believe it will be with our great national parks and forest reservations. There will be a period of indifference on the part of the rich, sleepy with wealth, and on the toiling millions, sleepy with poverty, most of whom never saw a forest; a period of screaming protest and objection from the plunderers, who are as unconscionable and enterprising as Satan. But light is surely coming, and the friends of destruction will preach and bewail in vain.

The axe and saw are insanely busy, chips are flying thick as snowflakes, and every summer thousands of acres of priceless forests, with their underbrush, soil, springs, climate, scenery, and religion are vanishing away in clouds of smoke, while, except in the national parks, not one forest guard is employed. . . .

Any fool can destroy trees. They cannot run away; and if they could, they would still be destroyed — chased and hunted down as long as fun or a dollar could be got out of their bark hides, branching horns, or magnificent bole backbones. Few that fell trees plant them; nor would planting avail much towards getting back anything like the noble primeval forests. During a man's life only saplings can be grown, in the place of the old trees — tens of centuries old — that have been destroyed. It took more than three thousand years to make some of the trees in these Western woods — trees that are still standing in perfect strength and beauty, waving and singing in the mighty forests of the Sierra. Through all the wonderful, eventful centuries since Christ's time — and long before that — God has cared for these trees, saved them from drought, disease, avalanches, and a thousand straining, leveling tempests and floods; but he cannot save them from fools — only Uncle Sam can do that.

191